CHAPLAIN TO MR SPEAKER
The Religious life of
the House of Commons

HMSO publications are available from:

HMSO Publications Centre
(Mail and telephone orders only)
PO Box 276, London SW8 5DT
Telephone orders 071-873 9090
General enquiries 071-873 0011
(queuing system in operation for both numbers)

HMSO Bookshops
49 High Holborn, London, WC1V 6HB   071-873 0011 (Counter service only)
258 Broad Street, Birmingham, B1 2HE   021-643 3740
Southey House, 33 Wine Street, Bristol, BS1 2BQ   (0272) 264306
9–21 Princess Street, Manchester, M60 8AS   061-834 7201
80 Chichester Street, Belfast, BT1 4JY   (0232) 238451
71 Lothian Road, Edinburgh, EH3 9AZ   031-228 4181

HMSO's Accredited Agents
(see Yellow Pages)

and through good booksellers

HOUSE OF COMMONS
LIBRARY DOCUMENT No. 19

General Editor: C C Pond

CHAPLAIN TO MR SPEAKER

The Religious life of the House of Commons

Donald Gray

*Chaplain to the Speaker
of the House of Commons*

LONDON: HMSO

'The use now is that the
Speaker have a Chaplain,
and comes to the House
and reads the prayer'.

Observations, Rules and Orders
of the House of Commons,
Ambrose Kelly, 1685.

Contents

Foreword

by the Rt Hon Bernard Weatherill MP
Speaker of the House of Commons

IN MAY 1901 THE EDITOR OF *HANSARD* WROTE TO *THE Times* on the subject of the House of Commons' Prayers. After very briefly describing their history he concluded by venturing to suggest that 'this is one of those by-paths of history well worth exploring, whose exploration must be the work of the enthusiast and the specialist'. Mr O'Shaughnessy thought that Canon Wilberforce, who was at that time Chaplain to the Speaker, 'if he would find or make the time would give us a charming booklet on the subject'. It seems he never did, so I am personally delighted that ten Speakers and ten Chaplains later, my Chaplain, Dr Donald Gray, has found, or made, the time to undertake the task.

The prayers which are said before we commence our daily proceedings are the subject of an often repeated 'chestnut'—that the Chaplain enters the Chamber, looks at the Members and prays for the Nation. I do, however, assure readers that prayers are taken very seriously by Members and are considered by many to be an essential part of the day's proceedings. Indeed it should be noted that we spend as much time each week in prayer as we do over Prime Minister's Questions.

However, the daily prayers, as Dr Gray explains, are only part of the duties of the Chaplain and of the religious life within the Palace of Westminster. I hope this Library Document will make more people aware of the fact that at the very heart of our democratic processes there is convergence of Church and State which is valued and highly respected.

Acknowledgements

ON MANY OCCASIONS SINCE THE RT HON. BERNARD Weatherill did me the honour of inviting me to be his Chaplain, I have been asked about the origins both of the office of Speaker's Chaplain and of the prayers with which the House of Commons commences its proceedings each day. So it was a happy chance when Dr David Menhennet, the Librarian of the House of Commons, asked me if I would undertake the task of writing a history of the office for the series of Library Documents of which he was until 1990 General Editor.

That initial enthusiasm of Dr Menhennet was matched by Sir John Sainty, then Clerk of the Parliaments, who is also a distinguished historian, and he generously shared with me the researches he had commenced on a list of Speaker's Chaplains. However, very little would have been possible without the courteous and skilled help of the staff of the Commons Library, particularly those who work in the Oriel Room. For all their assistance I am immensely grateful.

There are others in the Palace of Westminster who have taken an interest in this project and who have either made useful suggestions for possible lines of investigation, or have produced documents of which I would not otherwise have been aware. For help in this way I wish to record my thanks to Sir Clifford Boulton, the Clerk of the House, Sir Alan Urwick, Serjeant at Arms, and Sir John Gingell, Gentleman Usher of the Black Rod.

My thanks are also due for all the assistance I have received from the Westminster Abbey Library through Mrs Enid Nixon and Dr Richard Mortimer. My secretary, Pamela Carrington, has very kindly spent many hours of her own time proof reading the text.

A number of Cathedral and University libraries have been diligent in producing photographs and other illustrations which were not available elsewhere. In response to my enquiries, a number of Bishops and Deans have involved themselves in detective work on behalf of this research. I would wish to thank the Bishops of Chester, Oxford and Worcester and the Deans of Durham, Lichfield, Ripon, Rochester, Lincoln and Worcester. With their help it has been possible to gather together a most fascinating "Rogues' Gallery" containing many of my predecessors.

I am pleased to be able to acknowledge the help given me by the libraries at Lambeth Palace, St Deiniol's Harwarden, the Athenaeum, Liverpool, the Church Commissioners and the Norfolk Record Office.

The task of preparing all the material for the printer was made easier than it would otherwise have been by the skills of Dr Chris Pond (new General Editor), whose support and interest I have very much valued. To Fred Stubbs of HMSO Graphic Design belongs all the credit for the splendid design of this book.

I am very grateful to the following for permission to reproduce illustrations: The Dean and Chapter of Ripon, for Webber; the Durham University Library for Smith; the Manuscript Dept., Duke University Library, Durham, North Carolina (Charles Moss Collection), for Grenville's letter to Charles Moss; to David Tredinnick, Esq. MP for the baptism scene; to the Lord Bishop of Oxford, and the Church Commissioners of England for the Moss portrait, and to them and the Lord Bishop of Chester for that of Gastrell; to the Master and Fellows of Trinity College Cambridge for Wordsworth; to the Dean and Chapter of Worcester for Onslow. Many of the Staff of these institutions gave freely of their time and took much trouble in the production and copying of material: we are most grateful to them.

Once again my wife, Joyce, has 'borne the burden and heat of the day' (and often of the night) as she has typed and retyped these pages in their many stages of drafting. Without her painstaking efforts this work would not have appeared. My daughter, Clare Thornton-Reid, helped with the compiling of the index.

There could be no better person to contribute the foreword to this book than Mr Speaker himself. I appreciate his enthusiastic willingness to do so.

I can only hope and trust that through these pages I have managed to answer some of those questions and queries that I have been asked over the past few years. Also my wish is to convey something of the responsibility that all those of us who have been called to exercise this ministry are bound to feel as we go about our work within the Palace of Westminster.

Donald Gray
October 1990

Abbreviations

Al. Cant. (1) – J. & J. A. Venn, *Alumni Cantabrigienses to 1751*, 1922–27

Al. Cant. (2) – J. A. Venn, *Alumni Cantabrigienses 1752–1900*, 1940–54

Al. Oxon. (1) – Joseph Foster, *Alumni Oxonienses 1500–1714*, 1891

Al. Oxon (2) – Joseph Foster, *Alumni Oxonienses 1715–1886*, 1891

Athenae Ox. – Anthony à Wood, (new ed. Philip Bliss), *Athenae Oxonienses*, 1813–1820

BCR – *Brasenose College Register 1509–1909*, Oxford Historical Society, vol. LV, 1909

Bio. Brit. – *Biographia Brittanica or the lives of those who have flourished in Great Britain & Ireland from the earliest Ages down to the present Times*, 1747–1766

Burke LG – *Burke's Genealogical and Heraldic History of the Landed Gentry*

Burke Peer. – *Burke's Peerage and Baronetage*

Cant. Acts – Archbishop of Canterbury's Acts Books, Lambeth Palace Library

Cantuar – Edward Carpenter, *Cantuar: The Archbishops in their Office*, 1971

CCR – *City and Court Register*

CEYB – *Church of England Year Book*

Chadwick – Owen Chadwick, *The Victorian Church*, 1966, 1970

CJ – *Commons Journals*

Clergy List – *The Clergy List*

Crockford – *Crockford's Clerical Directory*

CSYB – *Civil Service Year Book*

CSPD – *Calendar of State Papers (Domestic)*

Cust – Lionel Cust, *Records of the Cust Family*, series III, 1927

d – ordained deacon (date)

DECH – Ed. S. L. Ollard, Gordon Crosse, Maurice F. Bond, *Dictionary of English Church History*, 3rd ed., 1948

Denison – Viscount Ossington, *Notes from my Journal when Speaker of the House of Commons, John Evelyn Denison*, 1900

DGB – William L. R. Cates, *A Dictionary of General Biography*, 4th ed., 1885

Don – *Diaries of A. C. Don*. Lambeth Palace Library: 1931–46, *WAM*: 1947–53

DNB – Ed. Leslie Stephens & Sydney Lee, *Dictionary of National Biography*, 1885–1901

Eton Reg. (1) – Wasey Strong, *The Eton College Register 1441–1698*, 1943

Eton Reg. (2) – R. A. Austen-Leigh, *The Eton College Register 1698–1790*, 1921 & 1927

Eton List – H. E. C. Stapylton, *The Eton College Lists from 1791–1850*, 1864 and 1868

Fasti Rip. – *Memorials of the Church of SS Peter and Wilfrid Ripon vol. II*, Publications of the Surtees Society, vol. LXXVIII, 1886

Fasti Ox. – Anthony à Wood, *Fasti Oxonienses*, 1820

Fasti Wynd. – S. L. Ollard, *Fasti Wyndesorienses: The Dean and Canons of Windsor*, 1950

FEA – J. Le Neve (completed by T. Duffy Hardy), *Fasti Ecclesiae Anglicanae*, 1854

FEH – Henry Cotton, *Fasti Ecclesiae Hibernicae: The succession of the prelates and members of the Cathedral bodies in Ireland*, 1849

FES – William Henry Jones, *Fasti Ecclesiae Sarisberiensis*, 1879 & 1881

GEC – *The Complete Peerage of England, Scotland and Ireland, Great Britain and the United Kingdom*, 1910–1959

GM – *Gentleman's Magazine*, 1731–1907

GS – *Grammar School*

Guardian – *Guardian* (weekly Church Newspaper, 1846–1951)

Harrow (1) – W. T. J. Gun, *The Harrow School Register, 1571–1800*, 1934

Harrow (2) – R. Courtenay Welch, *The Harrow School Register, 1801–1893*, 1894

HCCR – House of Commons, Chaplain's Room

Hearne – Ed. C. E. Doble, *Remarks and Collections of Thomas Hearne*, 1885

Hist. Reg. – *The Historical Register*, 1717–1739

HLRO – House of Lords Record Office

KS – King's Scholar, Westminster School

Lit. Anec. – J. Nichols, *Literary Anecdotes*, 1812–15

Luttrell – Narcissus Luttrell, *A Brief Historical Relation of State Affairs from September 1678 to April 1714*, 1857

Marlborough – *Marlborough College Register, 1834–1904*, 5th ed., 1905

matric. – matriculated

MEB – Frederick Boase, *Modern English Biography*, 1892, and Supplement

Nov. Rep. – George Hennessey, *Novum Repertorium
   Ecclesiasticum Parochiale Londinense,* 1898
N & Q – *Notes and Queries.* From 1849 to date

ODCC (ed. 2) Ed. F. L. Cross and E. A. Livingstone,
   Oxford Dictionary of the Christian Church, 2nd ed. revised,
   1984
p – ordained priest (date)
PC – Priest-in-Charge

Rep. Eccl. – Richard Newcourt, *Repertorium Ecclesiasticum
   Parochiale Londinense,* 1708 & 1710
RK – Royal Kalendar
ROW – G. F. Russell Barker and Alan H. Stenning, *The
   Record of Old Westminsters, a biographical list of all those who
   are known to have been educated at Westminster School from
   the earliest time to 1927,* 1928
   J. B. Whitmore and G. R. Y. Radcliffe, *A supplementary
   volume to "The Record of Old Westminsters",* n.d.

trans. – translation

Trinity – W. W. Rouse Ball and J. A. Venn, *Admissions to
   Trinity College Cambridge, 1546–1900, 1911–1916*

VCH – Victoria County History, 1900–

WAR – Joseph Lemuel Chester, *The Marriage, Baptismal,
   and Burial Registers of the Collegiate Church or Abbey of St
   Peter Westminster,* 1876
WAM – Westminster Abbey Archives in Abbey Library and
   Muniment Room.
Welsby – Paul Welsby, *The Deans of Rochester 1542–1977,*
   1983. Copy in Rochester Cathedral Library
Win. Schol. – Thomas Frederick Kirby, *Winchester Scholars. A
   List of the Wardens, Fellows and Scholars of St Mary College
   of Winchester, near Winchester, commonly called Winchester
   College,* 1888
Wordsworth – Charles Wordsworth, *Annals of My Early Life
   1806–1846,* 1891
WW – *Who's Who*
WWW – *Who Was Who*

GRAPHIC AND DAILY GRAPHIC SKETCHES.

PEACEFUL PRELIMINARIES.

Archdeacon Farrer, with Speaker Peel, about to commence prayers. "Members go through their devotions in severe solitude. There are, however, commanding the House, one or two glass doors, and placed behind one of these a privileged onlooker can observe the scene."
Drawing by Reginald Cleaver in Reginald Cleaver and others. *Parliamentary Pictures and Personalities [. . .] 1890–1893* (pub. 1893), p 7.

Part One

Chapter One

Chapels and Chaplains at Westminster

ALTHOUGH BOTH OXFORD AND LINCOLN CAN CLAIM to take precedence over the metropolis as places selected for the holding of the earliest known Parliaments, it belongs to Westminster to claim the distinction of having witnessed the full dawn of the English Constitution.

Westminster had been the main residence of the sovereign since the time of Edward the Confessor[1] and he had added to the dignity of *Villa Westmonasterii* by his building[2] of the Benedictine Abbey of St Peter at his Palace gates. After the Conquest, William the Conqueror deliberately held his coronation in the church which the saintly Edward had built and in which he had been buried in 1066, in order to ingratiate himself with his new subjects and to clearly associate himself in their minds with the dead Saint and King. Thus Westminster, by virtue of the royal force of gravity, drew to itself first Parliament, later the Exchequer, and eventually, all the offices of government.

As the present task is the detailing of the arrangements that have been made for the religious observances of the House of Commons throughout its history, it must be remembered that from the outset of its location in Westminster, Parliament has found itself surrounded by reminders of the call to Christian worship and devotion. Not only by the near presence of the Abbey, but also by the chapels which existed in the Palace of Westminster. Edward the Confessor had a chapel within the Palace dedicated to St John the Evangelist[3] and it is said that it was King Stephen who added another, which he dedicated to his patron Saint, the Christian proto-martyr, St Stephen[4].

The re-building of St Stephen's
In the Middle Ages building was the way in which the aristocrat demonstrated his influence and importance. In 1245 aristocratic circles in Western Europe were greatly impressed by the building which Louis IX of France undertook of the very latest and most fashionable type of private chapel – Sainte Chapelle in Paris. Henry III went to France to join in the ceremonies and celebrations surrounding the consecration of the Chapel, but hurried back to England in order to rebuild Westminster Abbey in a fashion which he believed would surpass even Sainte Chapelle.

King Louis possessed a precious relic of the Crown of Thorns around which he had wished to build his chapel. Interestingly, it was an earlier relic of the Kings of France that provided the name for the particular type of building designed to contain such objects of devotion. It is also the derivation of part of the title of the office under examination in this work.

The Kings of France had as a sacred possession what they piously believed to be part of the cloak which the soldier-saint Martin had divided with his sword when he had been asked for alms by a ragged beggar[5]. The Latin for a cape or cloak is *cappa*, and the building in which the relic was preserved was the *capella* (hence 'chapel'). This in turn provided the title for the priest whose duty it was to guard the relic, he was *capellanus* which became 'chaplain'[6].

King Henry of England knew that he had more than just a fragment of material, however revered, in the church which was just outside his palace. He had the body of the saintly king from whom he and his immediate predecessors claimed succession to the throne of England. Consequently he set about the rebuilding of the Abbey in such a way that it would surpass Sainte Chapelle and would give all due honour to Edward the Confessor.

The Sainte Chapelle.
Drawn by T.S. Boys, 1836.

It was this same desire to build and impress that inspired the endeavours of his son, Edward I. Although he is often remembered as the builder of the many castles that his troubled reign necessitated, Edward should never be forgotten at Westminster for his rebuilding of the chapel in the Palace there.

If the rebuilding of the Abbey by Henry III was inspired by the prestigious elegance of Sainte Chapelle in Paris in which his royal brother-in-law, Louis, now worshipped, it must be admitted that King Edward's work at the Palace of Westminster was even more obviously architecturally imitative.

The chapel in Paris was neither a great cathedral nor an abbey, it was indeed a private chapel, but a private chapel *par excellence*. It was built in what has been called the *Seigneurial* style, but this chapel did not inaugurate that style, it had already been adopted in a number of places earlier that century[7]. The essential feature of this type of chapel consisted of, what was in effect, putting one building on top of another. It was an arrangement which can be seen to derive from the long-standing custom of living in the upper storey of a farmhouse while stalling the animals underneath. Thus the *Seigneur* and his family occupied the upper storey while the animals and servants lived below. When this principle was adapted to accommodate religious functions it became a church in which the lord was able to hear Mass in the room above, while the lesser orders had to be content with worshipping in the lower part of the same building. It was such an arrangement that obtained at Sainte Chapelle and so Edward I decided that he would demolish what he had now come to be convinced were the old-fashioned Romanesque buildings of his predecessors, in order to provide for this new, modern, and more fashionable, conception.

Work began on 20 April 1292 and the result is acknowledged to have been a gothic masterpiece and to have been the architectural precursor of what is known as the Perpendicular Style[8].

The work was by no means complete by the death of Edward I in 1307, nor even at the death twenty years later of Edward II, although the Undercroft had probably been completed in 1323. The roof was finally put on in the reign of Edward III in 1346. Painting and decorating continued for the best part of a further twenty years[9].

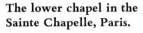

The lower chapel in the Sainte Chapelle, Paris.

The foundation of the College of St Stephen

In 1348 a decision was taken that was to have the effect of decisively affecting the way in which the House of Commons was to conduct its business in a period still many years hence. This occurred when Edward III decided to found two colleges of priests to pray for him and his family. One of these was to be at Windsor Castle (now known as the Queen's Free Chapel of St George) and the other would be at the Palace of Westminster in the already existing St Stephen's Chapel. The College which the King founded at Westminster was to consist of a Dean and twelve secular canons, with twelve vicars, four clerks and six choristers for whom the King assured an income of £500[10].

Of this College at Westminster Edward said, in the instrument in which he founded the College, that he was doing it in honour of St Stephen, the first Christian martyr, but also that he had in mind the honouring of the blessed Mary[11]. This fact helps to explain the dedication of the Undercroft to St Mary, which title the remaining part of the Chapel retains to this day (it is sometimes latinised to *S. Maria sub volta*.)

The restoration of the Undercroft

Before leaving the matter of the two-storey *Seigneurial* design of St Stephen's Chapel, this is a convenient place to point out the historical incorrectness of the more recent custom of referring to the Undercroft as 'the Crypt Chapel'. It will be realised from what has just been described that, although the Chapel is now reached by descending steps, it is *not* a crypt but the site of the medieval ground floor of the chapel of which the upper floor was destroyed in the fire of 1834. The whole chapel was the Collegiate Chapel of St Stephen, the Undercroft was its Lady Chapel.

Although the nineteenth century fire harmed much of the stonework, the Undercroft Chapel was sufficiently undamaged to be retained and restored. The exterior stonework was refaced and repaired by Sir Charles Barry, the architect to the New Palace, in 1858–9. The bulk of the restoration, however, was the work of his son, E. M. Barry, between 1860 and 1870. The chapel was richly painted by F. and G. J. Crace, whose firm had worked from the first with Augustus Pugin and Charles Barry in the restoration of the Palace[12].

The dissolution of the College of St Stephen

Although some changes in the religious practices of the day were allowed by Henry VIII, it is often forgotten that the majority came after his death. However, in the matter of the dissolution of the major religious houses the King was zealously involved during his life-time. Yet he was not inclined to alter arrangements for his own Royal College in the Palace of Westminster, even though York Place (Whitehall Palace) had been, since the deprivation of Cardinal Wolsey in 1529, his preferred residence in London. It was left to his son Edward VI, or Somerset acting for him, to see that *The Second Chantries Act* in 1547 dissolved the College of St Stephen[13]. The buildings and gardens of the College were given to Sir Ralph Fane but the Chapel of St Stephen was assigned to the House of Commons.

From its earliest days until this particular time, the House of Commons, somewhat surprisingly, had not possessed any permanent home of its own. It had met variously in Westminster Hall, in the Refectory of Westminster

St Stephen's Chapel.
John Nalson, *Impartial Collection*, 1684. (Bodleian Library)

A Conjectural reconstruction of the interior of St Stephen's Chapel.
(Maurice Hastings, *St Stephen's Chapel and its place in the development of Perpendicular style in England*, 1955.)

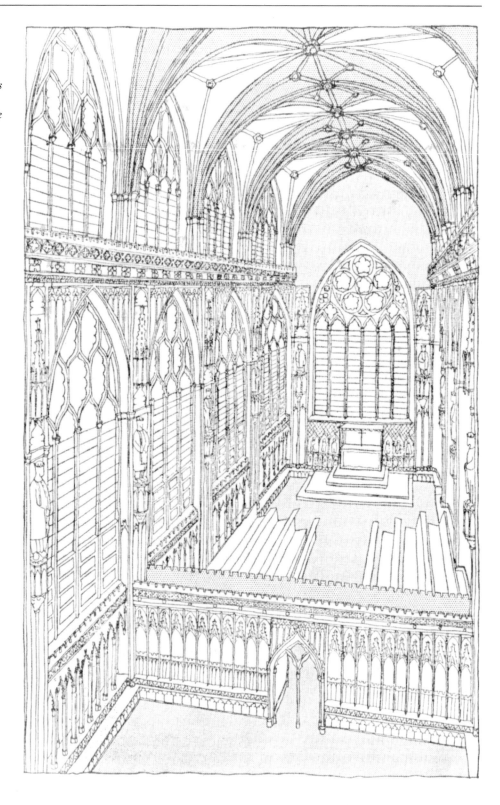

Abbey and in the Chapter House there. Now, by the King's gift, the Commons was able to settle into a regular place of meeting of its own. But what they settled into was a building of a particular character. Although it was no longer an active place of worship, the fact that for just short of two hundred years it had been a collegiate church meant, as has been previously

A section through St Stephen's Chapel which shows how the House of Commons, after the seventeenth century, was fitted inside the existing walls of the Chapel (From E W Brayley and J Britton, *History of the Ancient Palace and the late Houses of Parliament at Westminster, 1836.*)

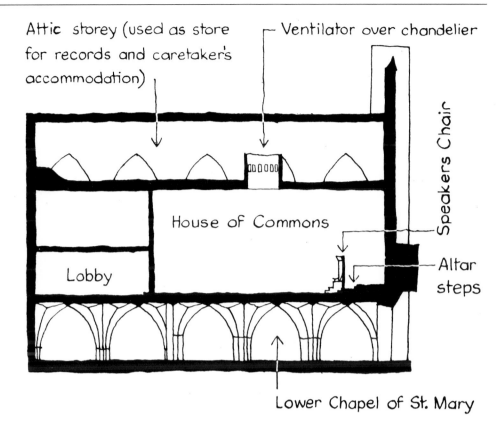

Attic storey (used as store for records and caretaker's accommodation)

Ventilator over chandelier

Speakers Chair

House of Commons

Lobby

Altar steps

Lower Chapel of St. Mary

hinted, that the furnishings of the building imposed upon the assembling members a pattern of seating which has in turn determined the style of debate right down to this present day[14]. And furthermore, the House has twice in the recent past – following the 1834 fire and then again after the 1941 bombing – consciously decided to retain this pattern[15]. These decisions kept the ecclesiastical and collegiate style of seating in contrast to the semi-circular arrangements of all other assemblies, with the notable exception of those Commonwealth parliaments which have retained this particular "Westminster" model. When the Commons assembles, it adopts the seating arrangements of the collegiate body whose place of worship their parliamentary forefathers inherited over four hundred and fifty years ago.

Chapter Two

Prayers in the House of Commons

S URROUNDED AS THEY WERE BY SO MANY REMINDERS OF a Christian heritage, it is not altogether surprising that the House of Commons should choose to maintain a tradition of asking God's blessing and guidance on its deliberations. Equally it was perhaps inevitable that they would eventually have a duly-appointed Chaplain whose task it would be to lead them in a daily act of worship and to perform for them such other religious duties as from time to time might be necessary.

It has already been noted that before 1547 the meetings of the House of Commons had taken place in various buildings in Westminster. The locations were all either in the Palace of Westminster or within the cloisters of the adjacent Benedictine monastery[1]. As we have seen, in those early days there were, in the Palace, ample opportunities for worship and devotion on either of the levels of the Collegiate Church of St Stephen. Nearby, in the monastery of St Peter, the full round of offices according to the rule of St Benedict was maintained and each day up to 50 priest brothers[2] would be offering their Mass in the Abbey Church. This is not to take into account the worship which took place in St Margaret's Church, which had been provided by the

View of Westminster by Wenceslaus Hollar, 1647.

Westminster Monks, probably as early as the 11th Century, for the people of Westminster, 'in order to remove a potentially disruptive lay congregation from their midst'[3].

With such an array of public and private devotion readily available in those earlier days, it would perhaps seem to us that there was little necessity to arrange any specific act of worship for the House of Commons. However, the spirituality of the age would have inclined towards the offering of votive masses for the special intention of God's guidance on the deliberations of the assembled House[4].

The offering of a mass or, more rarely, attendance at a monastic office, would have been the only options available – no other liturgical form would, at that time, have been thought to be adaptable to this purpose. Anything remotely like the seventeenth century form of prayers which has now long served the Commons for their devotions, let alone today's special service compilations, would have been quite unknown to any priest (conventual or secular) living in any of the centuries between the twelfth and the sixteenth.

It must also be remembered that in this early period of Parliamentary history its meetings were not the semi-continuous event of the present day. While between 1339 and 1399 a Parliament was summoned to Westminster almost every year between 1400 and 1509, the rate was cut by half and only seven Parliaments were convened between 1510 and 1540[5]. It was hardly a pattern which necessitated rigid unalterable provisions for prayer, certainly not the appointment of a priest with carefully designated parliamentary duties.

Westminster Abbey and St Margaret's Church by T Bowles, 1753.

There is evidence available that as early as the reign of Edward II, in the early 1320's, it was customary to open a new session of Parliament with a

sermon in the Abbey. This would have been an assembly of both houses together[6]. When Parliament was in session on a holy day members would attend the monastic office of Prime in the Abbey before beginning the day's work[7]. By the reign of Richard III the custom of opening a new session with a sermon in the Abbey seems to have been well-established. It is known that the Parliament of 1483 was opened with a sermon preached by the Lord Chancellor (Bishop Russell), and in writing of the opening of Parliament, Gairdner states that the preaching of a sermon was done according to custom[8].

However, by the time that the Commons moved into its own permanent chamber in the disused Collegiate Chapel of St Stephen, many things had changed in both Church and State.

In the first place, the College of priests in the Palace had now been dispersed, as had the monks of Westminster; but more importantly a very different religious tone was now abroad. The Church of England had by now adopted many of the ideas from continental protestantism. Yet, even so, it had not thrown off entirely all links with historic Catholic usages: instead it had subjected many of those ancient traditions to critical examination, and, in that light, changes and reforms had been made. In particular, the necessity of channelling all prayer through the Mass and consequently the necessity of the presence of a priest for any public act of prayer was now questioned. The concept of 'The priesthood of all believers' shaped the devotions of those who had been influenced by the new theology. This meant that the necessity of a readily available clergyman did not need to inhibit the House of Commons from having prayers when it assembled, even if there were only lay members present in the House. Indeed, in keeping with the religious mood of the time, prayer, not least extempore prayer, was believed to be a highly desirable prelude to any meeting, particularly when many ecclesiastical and doctrinal matters formed the agenda for the meetings of Parliament in those days.

The establishment of the custom
The first detailed reference to prayers being said actually in the Commons chamber itself[9] occurs in the first year of the reign of Elizabeth I. The *Commons Journal* for 11 February 1558 records:

> 'This morning Litany was said by the Clerk kneeling and answered by the whole House on their knees with diverse prayers'[10].

It may be speculated that the practice of daily prayers became established about this time – whether before this date or soon after cannot be said, as there is no record which gives us the precise details. Prayers would seem to have been said in the Parliament of 1563–67 because on the opening day of the next Parliament (4 April 1571) the Journal records the House's agreement:

> that the Litany shall be read every day in this House during this Parliament as in the last was used; and also a prayer by Mr. Speaker such as he shall think fittest for this time, to be begun every day at half hour after eight of the clock in the morning and that each one of this House then making default shall forfeit for every time 4d to the Poormen's box'[11].

This was in the Speakership of Sir Christopher Wray, and it is said that the House over which he presided was in the main a Puritan assembly[12], which would have favoured extempore prayer for the Speaker's contribution.

A little light is cast upon parliamentary custom at this time, when Thomas

Norton; who was a member of the House of Commons of 1571 and then of the 1572–83 Parliament, as a member for London and was also City Remembrancer[13], called upon the Lord Mayor of London in 1574 to prepare a scheme of procedure for the Court of Aldermen and the Common Council. In his paper to the Lord Mayor, Norton suggested that the proceedings of both these bodies should be opened with prayer. He wrote:

> 'I could gladly wish that some form of prayer might daily be used in your court and council chamber by you and all your brethren before you enter into causes. It is so used in the Parliament, and though such use be but of late, I trust it shall be continued, and grow to be old'[11].

The phrase 'though such use be but of late', from this contemporary source, is of great interest. Norton's wish, that Parliament should continue the practice of prayers, was in fact realised, and from the reign of Elizabeth the custom obtained that the Clerk said the Litany and then the Speaker offered a special prayer[15]. The later introduction of a clergyman to say prayers was not universally popular, not least to the Clerk of the House. In a rather dry note in the *Journal* for 23 March 1603 the Clerk (who was at that time Fulk Onslow[16]) recorded that the prayers on that day had been read by the Clerk of the House 'to whose place the service anciently belongs'[17].

There is a small foretaste of things to come when in 1584 it is recorded:

> '*Ordered.* That a particular form of prayer be directed by some of this House for God's blessing and especially upon that day's consultation'[15].

It would seem that this resolution was not acted upon at that time, as no 'form of prayer' from that date is extant.

The use of a clergyman

Towards the end of Elizabeth's reign in 1597, Sir Simonds d'Ewes records what proved to be only a temporary change in the prevailing custom of the Clerk and the Speaker conducting the prayers, when a Minister of Religion was brought into the House to read prayers[19]. In 1601 d'Ewes says the minister who read the prayers was paid £10, taken from the end of session collection made for the poor also from the 'fine' paid by those members who left the session early[20].

However it does not seem that during the next 20 years there was, as yet, a regular requirement for the attendance of a clergyman. The House's devotions continued to be in the hands of the Speaker and the Clerk.

The *Journal* for 20 November 1621 reads:

> 'This day about 9 of the clock Mr. Speaker came; and prayers said in the usual manner, first by the Clerk, and after by the Speaker'[21].

It is not until 1643 that the House returns to the possibility of obtaining the services of a clergyman. In that year the *Journal* records an order of the House 'that one of the ministers of the assembly shall be appointed to pray with the House every morning'. Presumably this referred to one of their own selves. But this does not seem to have worked, because on 12 July 1650 the first Cromwellian Parliament resolved:

> 'that the Governors of the College of Westminster do take care that some fit and able person or persons do attend *de diem in diem* to pray in Parliament, and that they give their attendance accordingly'[22].

John Pelling
Chaplain 1714–1715
Photo: reproduced from
Fasti Wynd.

A similar order was issued to the Governors of the School and Almshouse of Westminster in September 1654:

> 'that such of the morning Lecturers, as preacheth on the respective Days, do attend each Morning that they preach, to pray in this House'[23].

By an Act of Parliament in September 1649 the affairs of the College (i.e. Westminster Abbey) were finally put into the hands of fifty-six Governors, who ran it. The Governors arranged the preachers and lecturers who conducted the daily 'Exercise' which had replaced Matins and Evensong from 1643. It was from this number that the person who attended the House would come. He was not one of the Prebendaries – they had either fled or been excluded[24]. None the less it does provide the first link in a chain of continuing connection between the staff of the Collegiate Church and the Commons, complicated though that will be seen to have been. Neither of these arrangements worked very satisfactorily, and in Richard Cromwell's Parliament one minister, William Cooper of St Olave's Southwark[25], seems to have attended the House for prayers on a fairly regular basis. The House decided on 31 January 1659 that they desired William Cooper 'to continue to officiate and perform the duty of prayer in this House every morning during this session of Parliament'[26]. When that Parliament ended on 22 April 1659 the House resolved:

> 'that the sum of fifty pounds be given and bestowed on Mr Cooper, the minister, for his great labour and pains in attending the House daily' [27].

Thus William Cooper was the first clergyman to attend regularly to conduct prayers in the House of Commons. However, the appellation 'Chaplain' was not attached to him. Edward Bowles, however, was given the designation 'Chaplain' when he was appointed to accompany the twelve members of the House of Commons, who along with six members of the House of Lords and twenty 'honourable persons' were to attend upon King Charles II on the restoration of the Monarchy on 7 May 1660[28]. Bowles was a presbyterian minister[29] and there is no other record of him performing any other service to the House of Commons.

Fasting and Preaching

As we consider the religious practices of the House, we must note not only its spoken prayers but also its fasts and sermons. The first recorded mention of fasts and sermons for the House is in January 1581 when 'a motion was made for a public fast, with prayers and preaching'. The preacher on this occasion was to be nominated by those members who were Privy Counsellors and the event was to take place in the Temple Church.

There is no further mention of the subject of fasting and preaching until 1640. On November 17 the records say:

> 'Tuesday was the fast day which was kept piously and devoutly; Doctor Burgess and Master Marshall preached before the House of Commons at least 7 houres betwixt them upon Jere. 50.5 and 2 Chron. 2.3'[30].

Twelve days later the whole House received the Communion[31]. This very special aspect of religious devotion will be examined when the relationship between the House of Commons and St Margaret's Church is considered in detail[32].

North view of Westminster Abbey and St Margaret's Church, early 19th century (before 1822).

There was a further sermon on 8 August 1641, but no fasting was apparently associated with it.

> 'Sunday by six of the clock in the morning there was a sermon at St Margaret's Westminster, before both Houses: after which they sate in their own House in Parliament all the forenoon'[33].

It was a House of Commons which took its religion extremely seriously that was willing to attend Church before sessions which started as early as 6 a.m. or, on occasion, to listen to sermons which lasted for up to seven hours at a stretch.

After the Restoration, the House marked various days in the year (if they were in session) with a special sermon in St Margaret's. These were 5 November (Gunpowder Plot), 30 January (Martyrdom of Charles I), 29 May (Restoration of Charles II) together with the Accession Anniversary, and those General Fast and Thanksgiving Days which were appointed from time to time by Royal Proclamation.

That the House expected a high level of erudition from its preachers is revealed when, on 31 January 1700, the House resolved:

> 'That, for the future, no Person be recommended to preach before this House, who is under the dignity of a Dean in the Church, or hath taken his Degree of Doctor of Divinity'[34].

On 4 June 1742 the Chaplain of the House was excepted from this restriction[35], though the biographies provided later in this book reveal that the removal of that restriction was not often necessary, the Chaplains having frequently obtained a doctorate of divinity.

Attendance fluctuated a great deal, but the House continued to appoint preachers, to formally thank them and then to invite them to publish their sermons. The exception to this invitation was the Reverend William Stephens, Rector of Sutton, Surrey in 1770[36]. He seems to have been the reason that the House adopted its 1700 'dignity test' for preachers. He

The interior of St Margaret's Church (looking east)
Showing the old east window with the date 1692 (about half a century before the erection of the present window), the Communion table before the erection of the *basso relievo* of the Supper at Emmaus and several monuments now removed, as well as the original pew of the Speaker on the opposite side of the chancel from the old pulpit and reading desk. Engraving from early 18th century.

Royal Coat of Arms of King Charles II in St Margaret's Church.
Photo: WAM

'Songs of Praise from Parliament', programme made by BBC TV, February 1990.
The Speaker and Mrs Weatherill in the Speaker's Pew in St Margaret's.

preached on the Martyrdom of King Charles and his words came too near the bone. He told the Commons that the observation of that day was not intended out of any detestation of King's murder, but to be

> 'a lesson to other Kings and Rulers, how they ought to behave themselves towards their subjects, lest they should come to the same end'[37].

The sermon which was preached on this particular anniversary continued to cause homiletical problems. In 1772 it was even proposed that the sermon of that year's preacher should be burnt by the Common Hangman as containing 'arbitrary, tory, high-flown doctrines'[38].

The sermons preached for the House of Commons between 1660 and 1832 deserve a special study of their own. They were all preached at St Margaret's except on 12 March 1800 and 13 February 1801 when the Church was under repair and St John's was used instead[39], but there were two hundred and thirty two of them[35]!

Chapter Three

The appointment of Chaplains and their reward

THE OFFICE OF CHAPLAIN IS A PRODUCT OF THE Cromwellian Parliaments, asserts Josef Redlich[1]. It is certainly true that the first time that a clergyman was regularly present in the House to conduct prayers was in Richard Cromwell's Parliament in 1659, but the evidence seems to show that the first appointment of a Chaplain (and so called) was at the Restoration in 1660. The first person to be described as such is Edward Voyce. He makes his appearance in the *Journal* in this way. On 8 September 1660, in the expectation that the Parliament which had been assembled since 25 April of that year, was about to be prorogued, a resolution was adopted by the House in these words:

> '*Ordered*, that the members of the House who are of His Majesty's Privy Council are hereby desired to attend the King and humbly to recommend to his Majesty from this House Mr. Edward Voyce, Master of Arts, for some mark of his Majesty's favour in regard to his constant and diligent attendance upon this House ever since the beginning of this Parliament, as Chaplain'[2].

In the event, Parliament was not prorogued and continued in session until almost the end of the year. However, on the eve of its eventual dissolution (28 December 1660) the House voted the Chaplain £120 out of the Excise, as compensation for his services[3], rather than the ecclesiastical preferment which seems was being sought for him by the House in its resolution of 8 September. Certainly for the next 169 years, until the changes which came in the wake of the Reform Act of 1832, it was through the method of preferment to a notable ecclesiastical post that Parliament contrived to reward their Chaplain rather than by any direct financial means.

Chaplains and preferment

The fact was that no salary was paid to the Chaplain. While giving evidence to the 1833 Select Committee on the Establishment of the House, John Rickman, a former Speaker's Secretary and by that time Clerk Assistant[4], was asked 'How is the Chaplain of the House remunerated?' To which Rickman answered[5]:

> '*A   The Chaplain of the House is remunerated by means of an Address to the House of Commons at the end of the Session, requesting His Majesty to confer some dignity in the Church on the Chaplain of the House of Commons.*
>
> Q   Is that done?
>
> A   *Yes, and in order to guard against the contingency of Parliament being dissolved during the Recess, they annually vote the address, but it is effectual only once for each Chaplain.*

William Wyndham Grenville to Charles Moss, 26 January 1792, in the Charles Moss Papers, Manuscript Department, Duke University Library, Durham, North Carolina.
Moss (Chaplain 1789–1791) is enquiring about the vacancy in the Bishopric of Norwich caused by the death of George Horne. In the event, Charles Manners Sutton was appointed as Bishop and Moss became a Prebendary of Westminster in August 1792.
Photo: reproduced by permission of the Duke University Library.

Q   How long is it expected the Chaplain will serve?
A   *Three years; or in other words, there are two Chaplains for a Parliament, if it endures more than three years; the usual consequence of the address is a Stall at Westminster, at Canterbury, at Windsor, or at Christchurch, Oxford.*

Q   Has he a salary for his services?
A   *He has not; eight guineas a year are given as an allowance in lieu of stationery, and he has no other perquisites; this he receives from the Speaker, out of the Speaker's allowance, in lieu of stationery.*

Q   Are those four stalls reserved expressly for the Chaplain?
A   *No; whichever happens to become vacant is given to him.*

Q   Does it not happen that a Chaplain is Chaplain for several years in succession?
A   *Yes; I have known Chaplains serve longer than three years; I think I have known one serve five, and another four years.*

Q   The recommendation of the House is always attended to?
A   *Yes; I have traced it back as far as the reign of King William.*

Q   They remain on the list until there is a vacancy?
A   *Yes.*

The full details of how this was worked out practically can be seen from the biographical listing in Part Two[6]. In the first Parliament of William III the House was specific in its recommendation on behalf of its Chaplain, Thomas Manningham. It asked that 'the next prebend of Windsor or Westminster that should fall vacant' should be conferred upon him[7]. This duly came about when on 28 January 1693 Manningham was installed as a Canon of Windsor[8]. Although this form of specific recommendation was peculiar to the first of the post-Revolution Parliaments, in the eighteenth century and in the nineteenth up to 1833, a prebend came to be looked upon as the reward for the Chaplain of the House after about three years service. In that period sixteen of the Chaplains became Canons of Westminster, thirteen Canons of Windsor, eight went to Canterbury as Canons and seven to Christchurch, Oxford. William Galloway (Chaplain 1699) was the only

Folliott Cornewall (LEFT) **Chaplain 1780–1784, on the arm of his Registrar.**
Photo: reproduced from a picture at Hartlebury Castle, by kind permission of the Lord Bishop of Worcester and the Church Commissioners for England.

Robert Stevens (CENTRE) **Chaplain 1815–1818**
Photo: reproduced from a portrait in the Chapter Room in Rochester Cathedral by kind permission of the Dean and Chapter of Rochester.

Christopher Wordsworth (RIGHT) **Chaplain 1818–1819**
Photo: from an original in Trinity College, Cambridge, reproduced by kind permission of the Master and Fellows.

chaplain to go on to be a Canon of Worcester[9], and only Robert Stevens (Chaplain 1817) went straight to being a Dean[10]. Whereas, eight of the Chaplains subsequently became either Deans or Bishops, with Thomas Manningham (Chaplain 1690)[11] and Cornewall (Chaplain 1780)[12] being both. Christopher Wordsworth (Chaplain 1818), brother of the poet, 'broke the mould' when he went to become Master of Trinity College Cambridge[13].

Although, as we have seen, Westminster and Windsor received the largest number (83%), Canterbury received its share, particularly in the 18th century. This provoked an unkind comment from Sir Egerton Brydges. He said Canterbury was 'richer in inanimate than in animate attractions' and that

> 'The metropolitan church ought to have been the reposing place of genius and learning. It was the feasting and sleeping spot of Speaker's Chaplains and powerful noblemen's tutors. Dr. Wellfit, the Senior Prebendary, lately deceased, who was Chaplain to Sir Fletcher Norton[14], held his stall forty seven years'[15].

The end of 'an undignified practice'

The last of these recommendations for preferment was made to William IV in 1835 on behalf of Temple Frere[16] because, as a result of their enquiries, the Select Committee on the Establishment of the House had made a recommendation about the remuneration of the Chaplain. They were of the opinion that the practice of giving him a Prebendal Stall after three years service was 'highly objectionable' and recommended its discontinuance. 'By this mode', they said:

> 'Appointment to high and dignified offices in the Church become dependent, not upon the possession of distinguished learning or piety, but upon the exercise, for probably a period of three years, of the moderate duties required by the Chaplain of the House of Commons'[17].

In place of preferment, they recommended a salary of £200 a year. The various recommendations of the Select Committee were not wholeheartedly approved when the Committee reported to the Commons, because many of the officials of the House faced large cuts in their income after many years of service. That this was not so in the case of the Chaplain eased the proposals in respect of the changes in his method of remuneration. On the floor of the House in 1835, Joseph Hume agreed with the Select Committee's criticism of the existing system for rewarding the Chaplains, calling the appeals to the Crown on the Chaplain's behalf 'undignified'. After Hume had made his plea for reform, James Abercromby, who had only become Speaker in February of that year, following Speaker Manners-Sutton's eighteen years' occupation of the Chair, intervened in the debate in order to state that the appointment of the gentleman who was now his Chaplain 'had been made without any inducement being held to him of a prospect of preferment'[18]. His Chaplain was John Vane, who served him for both the Parliaments over which Abercromby presided[19] and who certainly did not receive a Prebendal Stall at the close of his term of office[20].

The last Chaplain for whom a recommendation was made was Temple Frere, the eighth and last of Speaker Manners-Sutton's Chaplains. Frere went to be a Prebendary of Westminster in 1838. He was also the last Chaplain to occupy these two offices in this order. When in 1891 F. W. Farrar became Chaplain he was already a Canon of Westminster[21].

F W Farrar
Chaplain 1890–1896
'He is not a great preacher, but he is very eloquent and a little florid; so that the shop-keeping church-goer likes to hear him. He is not a bad man of business, and he is an apostle of temperance. He is self-made and he looks as prosperous as any ordinary parson can fairly expect to be. He is a picture of comfortable piety!' (*Vanity Fair*, 10 October 1891)

Chapter Four

The task of the Chaplain in more recent times

IS THE CLERGYMAN WHO PRESIDES OVER PRAYERS DAILY in the House of Commons 'Chaplain to the House' or 'Chaplain to the Speaker'? As has been seen, in the initial reference in the *Journal* to the first officially appointed Chaplain, Voyce, the members referred to 'his constant and diligent attendance upon this House . . . as Chaplain'[1]. This first appointment does seem to have been made by the House as a whole, but when Henry Carpenter was chosen to succeed him, this was on the nomination of Speaker Turner[2] and the appointment has been done in this manner ever since. However, there has always been a clear understanding that the Speaker is making the appointment, on behalf of the House, of a clergyman who will be the *persona*[3] for the Commons. This point was made in 1770 when Sir Fletcher Norton decided not to continue the appointment of William Barford, who had been appointed by his predecessor Sir John Cust, but instead had chosen Charles Burdett as Chaplain. A contributor to *The Gentleman's Magazine* on Barford's death in 1792 recalled the circumstances:

> 'Barford . . . appointed by Sir John Cust but did not continue above one session, Sir Fletcher Norton having made choice of another clergyman, and it was suspected that there was a design to prevent his being favoured with the customary recompense for his service. His friends, however, and many respectable friends he had, contended that he was not to be considered as chaplain of the Speaker, but of the House; and Mr. Thomas Townshead moved May 9 to address the King to confer upon Mr Barford as chaplain some dignity in the church'[4].

The fact has been somewhat obscured, not only by the customary title 'Chaplain to the Speaker', but also by the fact that the Chaplain has long been regarded as part of the Speaker's staff. In fact, at the time of the 1833 Select Committee, the Speaker's Department consisted simply of the Speaker's Secretary and the Speaker's Chaplain[5].

Since those days, the size of the Speaker's Department has grown, but the Chaplain has remained part of the inner circle of the Speaker's 'personal staff'[6]. The intimate connection between the Speaker and Chaplain also has procedural consequences, as Arnold Wilson has explained:

> 'though he is, in effect, the Chaplain of the House of Commons, so thoroughly was the tenure of the Chaplaincy identified with the Speakership, that the Chaplain could not appear in the House of Commons for the performance of his duty when the Chair was vacant owing to the death or retirement of the Speaker, and equally so before the creation of the Deputy-Speaker, when the Speaker was detained from the Chair by illness'[7].

Henry Drury
Chaplain 1857–1863
HCCR

It has also come to be understood that the priest nominated by the Speaker, and accepted by the House, will, in addition to his obligations towards Members, also provide a pastoral ministry where desired or necessary for the large number of people employed within the Palace of Westminster, and recent appointments have been made in this understanding[8].

The House of Commons and St Margaret's

St Margaret's was built, as we have noted, probably as early as the 11th century 'for the greater honour and peace of the monks as of parishioners'[9] yet it has had a long connection with Parliament, in particular with the House of Commons. Although Parliament as a whole continued into the seventeenth century to attend the Abbey at the Opening of Parliament, nevertheless it was St Margaret's that was the Commons' Church. The first occasion that this was expressed was on Palm Sunday (16 April) 1614 when the House decided to attend the Church for a corporate Communion[10]. In a debate four days earlier,

St Margaret's Church
Etched by Preston from a
drawing by Pearson, 1810.

complaint had been made that 'in the Abbey they administered not common
bread'[11]. There is also a letter written by John Chamberlain to Sir Dudley
Carleton, who was then Ambassador at Venice, on 14 April in which he
detailed the House's hesitations about worshipping in the Abbey:

> '...Upon the motion of Sir James Parrat, Duncombe, and Master Fuller yt is
> resolved the house shall receive the communion together on Sunday next. The
> place was once agreed to be Westminster Church, but for feare of copes and
> wafer cakes, and such other important reasons yt is now altered to St Margarets
> and those three appointed sextans or overseers to note who be absent'[12].

This was all a reference to the fact that the Abbey had continued to use the
wafer bread ordered by the first Book of Common Prayer of 1549[13]. Although
the Royal Injunction of Elizabeth ten years later had also made this same
provision, the House was obviously of the opinion that the rubrics of the
Prayer Book for 1559 and the Canons of 1604 did not allow anything but

'common bread'[14]. It was accordingly resolved that the House should attend the Parish Church of St Margaret and that the Speaker should be entrusted with the choice of the preacher[15].

Although the *Journal* makes no reference over the next six years to further official attendance, *D'Ewes Journal* and the Parish Records contain details of such services[16]. There are many of these references both before and during the Commonwealth period. A former Rector of St Margaret's has written of the time just before the Civil War:

> 'To any priest who celebrates the divine mysteries at the altar of the Commons' Church, it must always be a moving thought that in this very Chancel the protagonists in the tragic conflict between Crown and Parliament that issued in our Civil War – Wentworth and Pym, Hampden and Falkland, Cromwell and Vane and Hyde – knelt, in a sacred fellowship transcending all personal and public animosities, to receive the most comfortable Sacrament of the Body and Blood of Christ'[17].

After the Restoration the *Journal* bears witness to the regular use of the Church by the Commons. It was when a gallery was built in the north aisle of St Margaret's in 1644 that for the first time a definite allocation of seats for members of the House was made[18]. In 1681, during building of a second gallery in the south aisle, the opportunity was taken to provide a special pew for the Speaker, a custom which is continued to this day[19]. As a recognition of the close connection which existed between the House and the Church, between 1647 and 1876 various grants were made for the repair and restoration of the Church[20]. It was Parliamentary money that in 1759 made possible the purchase of the beautiful east window which had originally formed part of the dowry of Catherine of Aragon[21].

Interior of St Margaret's Church, as seen from the East End (LEFT)
Engraving by J Kay and G Hawkins, 1804.

The Speaker in his Pew (RIGHT)
(Engraving by A Walker, *The Ornaments of Churches Considered*, 1761.)

The Right Hon.ble Arthur Onslow, Esq.r Speaker, in his SEAT in S.t Margarets Church Westminster, the Parochial Church of the COMMONS of Great Britain. 1760

The Chancel of St Margaret's Church
Engraving by J Kay and G Hawkins, 1804.

Although grants from public funds have long ceased to be voted by the House, in 1984 the Speaker of the House (the Rt Hon. Bernard Weatherill MP) launched a highly successful Restoration Appeal for St Margaret's which was widely supported by members, officers and staff of the House and enabled a programme of necessary repairs and restoration to be undertaken[22]. In this they were acting in the spirit of the eighteenth century historian who wrote of St Margaret's:

> 'This Church, in the Year 1735, was not only beautifully repaired, but the Tower thereof cased and mostly rebuilt, at the Charge of three thousand and five hundred Pounds, given by Parliament, in consideration of its being, as it were, a national church, for the use of the House of Commons'[23].

Speaker Weatherill with Canon Gray inspecting the restoration work on St Margaret's which has been made possible through the Speaker's Appeal.
Photo: Eric Roberts.

This 'national church, for the use of the House of Commons' was used regularly throughout the 17th and 18th century for the services held to commemorate the Gunpowder Plot, the Martyrdom of Charles I and the Restoration of the Monarchy. It was not until 1859 that these particular State Services were finally abolished[24]. The next occasion, after that abolition, on which the House attended St Margaret's in state was on Sunday 22 May 1887 when they assembled to give thanks to God for Queen Victoria's Golden Jubilee[25]. They also worshipped there in the year of the Queen's Diamond Jubiliee[26]. The preacher at that service was Dr Farrar (Chaplain 1891–6) who had just left St Margaret's on being appointed Dean of Canterbury, and returned for this special occasion. Farrar had the distinction of being the last preacher ever to be formally thanked by resolution of the House for a sermon[27].

On 11 November 1918, after Lloyd George had announced the signing of the Armistice and described its terms, the Prime Minister moved that the House should then adjourn to St Margaret's in order to pray. Of that occasion the Archbishop of Canterbury (Randall Davidson) wrote:

'I do not suppose there has ever been in our history a more significant recognition of the Divine Presence and aid than in this sudden attendance of the Houses at Divine Service in lieu of a Commons debate'[28].

The precedent of 1918 was followed on both 8 May and 15 August 1945, when this time it was Winston Churchill who led the Commons across the road to St Margaret's for a quickly organised service of thanksgiving. On these two latter occasions the House of Lords went to the Abbey, thus complying with their ancient traditions[29].

F W Farrar
Chaplain 1890–1896
HCCR

The Rector and the Chaplaincy

No doubt because of this long association of St Margaret's with the House of Commons, and the fact that for nearly twenty years now the Rector of St

Margaret's has also been Chaplain to the Speaker, it has been assumed, by some, that these two posts are co-terminus; but this is not the case, there is no necessary ecclesiastical or Parliamentary connection between them.

Although Kenrick (Chaplain 1729)[30] and Webber (Chaplain 1812)[31] were both, as Prebendaries of the Abbey, appointed by the Chapter to be in charge of the Church and Parish as 'Curates of St Margaret's' (the Dean and Chapter as a whole being the Rector), their appointment came *after* they had completed their period of service as Chaplain. So it was not until 1890 (and also after an Act of Parliament in 1840 which had annexed the Rectory to a Canonry)[32] that on the sudden death of Henry White, who in addition to being Speaker's Chaplain was Master of the Royal Chapel of the Savoy, that a Rector of St Margaret's was appointed Chaplain[33]. F. W. Farrar had already been Rector for fourteen years before his appointment as Chaplain to the

**James Webber
Chaplain 1812–1815**
Photo: reproduced from a portrait in Ripon Deanery (The Minster House) by kind permission of the Dean and Chapter of Ripon.

**Basil Wilberforce
Chaplain 1896–1916**
'He is a good defender of unpopular causes, and as a theologian is characterised by unusual humanity and breadth. As Chaplain to the House of Commons he is under the inexorable necessity of being in a certain place at a certain time every day during Session; but, apart from that, his Parliamentary labours are not intolerably severe.' (*Vanity Fair*, 6 January 1900)

Speaker, and when he left to become Dean of Canterbury in 1896[34] it was one of his capitular colleagues, Basil Wilberforce, who was invited by Speaker Gully to succeed him. But Canon Wilberforce held the Canonry, which at that time was attached to St John's, Smith Square, not St Margaret's, so the connection was not immediately continued[35].

We have to wait until the First World War for the next time when the two offices are held together. On the death of Wilberforce in 1916, W. H. Carnegie, who had been Rector of St Margaret's since 1913, was appointed Speaker's Chaplain. Carnegie made a substantial personal investment in the uniting of the posts in people's minds by continuing in office for twenty years – the longest occupancy of the office of Speaker's Chaplain[36]. Carnegie's successor as Rector, V. F. Storr, was not chosen as Chaplain[37] – instead the Archbishop of Canterbury's Senior Chaplain, A. C. Don, was appointed. However, Dr Don fortuitously became a Canon of Westminster and Rector of St Margaret's in 1941 and so the connection was re-established, although it proved to be only temporary.

When Dr Don became Dean of Westminster in 1946 there was another disassociation of the offices (which was to last for a further fifteen years) on the appointment of Prebendary Christopher Cheshire as Chaplain. Prebendary Cheshire, like Don on his appointment, was a Chaplain at Lambeth. Cheshire served from 1946 to 1955 and was succeeded by the Master of Charterhouse (Dr John McLeod Campbell)[38]. Then Michael Stancliffe, who had been Rector of St Margaret's since 1957, was appointed Chaplain in 1961 and served for eight years, but he was followed in the office of Chaplain by another Master of Charterhouse (T. S. Nevill)[39]. Nevill served until 1972 when David Edwards, who had already been Rector since 1970, was appointed by Speaker Lloyd as his Chaplain[40].

Since 1972 each of the Chaplains has been also Rector of St Margaret's, even though, after the passing of the *Westminster Abbey and Saint Margaret Westminster Act 1972*, this title of 'Rector' is only held by a member of the Chapter[41], 'for the purpose of style and designation but not for any other purpose'[42].

Michael Stancliffe (RIGHT)
Chaplain 1961–1969
HCCR

David Edwards (FAR RIGHT)
Chaplain 1972–1978
HCCR

The Speaker's Mace (detail from the stained glass window in memory of Speaker Fitzroy in St Margaret's Church).
Photo: B D R Fleming.

All this emphasises that the Speaker is completely free to appoint any clergyman he wishes to be his Chaplain, and if any Rector of St Margaret's is invited by the Speaker to occupy the office, he is equally free to accept or decline the office[43].

The Speaker's Choice

The freedom of the Speaker to appoint any Church of England clergyman to act as his Chaplain is clear from the evidence already given. On just a few occasions, this freedom has caused a slight *frisson* of parliamentary and ecclesiastical excitement.

The preference of Speaker Norton for James King over William Barford, his predecessor's choice, has already been mentioned[44]. Although the House of Commons considered Barford badly done by, and took the opportunity to emphasise his role as Chaplain *to the House*, they do not seem to have challenged the custom of the Speaker choosing that Chaplain.

The next time that any embarrassment seems to have occurred was in the nineteenth century when Speaker Brand decided not to continue Henry White when the new Parliament assembled in 1874. Brand had inherited White when he took over the chair from Denison in 1872 in the middle of the 1868–1874 Parliament, but he decided that he wished Francis Byng to be his Chaplain. The irony is that when Byng succeeded his brother as Earl of Stafford in May 1889, Speaker Peel invited White to return as his Chaplain. Unfortunately White died in office the following year.

The White/Byng case was quoted in an incident a few years later which caused a little fluttering in some ecclesiastical dovecotes. In the diary of Sir Courtenay Ilbert, who was Clerk of the House from 1902–21, there are the following entries in 1906:

> 'Archdeacon Wilberforce came to see me in a state of great perturbation, to ask whether I could supply him with a copy of the Report of 1833 on House of Commons Establishments'.

Lowther, the new Speaker, had evidently indicated that Wilberforce would not be reappointed, and had cited the case of Speaker Brand who declined to reappoint White, preferring Byng instead. Ilbert observes:

> 'I understand from the Serjeant at Arms that this step gave rise to a good deal of comment. Byng subsequently got into financial difficulties, and when Peel became Speaker, he reappointed White, who continued to be Chaplain until his death'.

Later Wilberforce received a note from the Prime Minister, Campbell-Bannerman, marked 'Secret', and containing the words '*sursum corda*' ('lift up your hearts'). Wilberforce told Ilbert that the Law Officers and some of the Cabinet had been very angry. 'Of course the archdiaconal Hebraist may be subject to some discount,' wrote Ilbert[45]. Speaker Lowther's own recollection of what he seems to have regarded as a somewhat tiresome business, confirms the details.

> 'One of my first duties was to appoint the Speaker's Chaplain, and here a slight hitch occurred. When I was first elected, in the previous year, I had written a diplomatic letter to the Chaplain, asking him to continue in the office, which he then held, until the conclusion of the Parliament, intending to replace Canon Wilberforce, with whom I had not an intimate or even a close acquaintance, by a dignitary of the Church with whom I was well acquainted

Francis Byng (RIGHT)
Chaplain 1874–1889
'A long time ago Mr Byng was fond of horse-racing and an admirer of the ladies. His opinions are of a lower Church than some think they might be, but he is an amiable man, full of piety and knowledge of the world, and he looks beautiful in his priestly dress.' (*Vanity Fair*, 18 October 1879)

Henry White
Chaplain 1869–1874 and 1889–1890
HCCR

Basil Wilberforce
Chaplain 1896–1916
HCCR

and who happened to also be admirably suited for the position. When, however, I intimated this desire to Canon Wilberforce, he resented it strongly and induced the Prime Minister to intervene on his behalf. Being naturally anxious to start the new Parliament on good terms with the Prime Minister, I did not feel that the matter was one which I could press very strongly, and I yielded to his representations. The Prime Minister pointed out that the claims of the Canon to a deanery were strong and that in all probability a deanery would fall vacant before the lapse of many months, and that whilst he (the Prime Minister) could give no promise, I could rest assured that the Chaplain's claims to preferment in the Church would not be overlooked. I accordingly appointed Canon Wilberforce. The sequel to this story was, that although on two occasions a deanery was offered to him, once by Sir Henry Campbell–Bannerman and once by Mr. Asquith (to whom I had confided what had taken place) the Canon declined the proffered preferment and remained on as Chaplain of the House and Archdeacon of Westminster until his death in 1915. He was a son of Bishop Wilberforce of Oxford and Winchester fame, an ardent teetotaller, in his youth a keen sportsman and steeplechase rider, an attractive preacher, and the holder of some strange views as to the future life. Towards the end of his life he suffered much from asthma and often found it impossible to fulfil his duties in the House of Commons. Sir Henry Campbell-Bannerman used occasionally to send me marked passages in the reports of the Canon's sermons where he had propounded some more than usually strange doctrine[46].

Wilberforce's own biographer tells none of this story[47]! As Speaker Lowther says, he had to wait until 1916 until he could appoint a Chaplain of his own choice, who was W. H. Carnegie.

The Parliamentary Church Council

When what was popularly known as 'the Enabling Act' came into force in 1921[48], and thereby gave official status to Parochial Church Councils, it was realised that its provisions would not suit the needs of St Margaret's Parish, which was by then almost entirely non-residential, yet having its continuing connection with the House of Commons. The Rector (Canon Carnegie) had been Speaker's Chaplain since 1916, and he was concerned that if the provisions of the Enabling Act were applied without modification, a Parochial Council would be constituted on which the House of Commons had little or no representation 'and which would not be likely therefore to promote the maintenance and development of the connection between the House and the Church'[49]. Carnegie and a Churchwarden wrote to all Members and said,

> 'The word 'resident' implies intimate connection of some kind with the particular parish, but in existing usage has not been limited to those who actually sleep in it. Bearing this fact in view the Archbishops of Canterbury and York, who under Article 16 of the Enabling Act are the authoritative interpreters of its provisions, have decided that Members of the House of Commons may, for the purposes of the Act, be considered to have the status of residents in the parish in which the House is situated. Members therefore, who belong to the Church of England, and feel so disposed, can, making the customary declaration, have their names inscribed on the electoral roll of St Margaret's[50].'

Nearly two hundred favourable replies were received and the names were placed on 'St Margaret's Parliamentary Parochial Roll'. At a subsequent meeting in February 1922, of those who had enrolled themselves, twenty-five

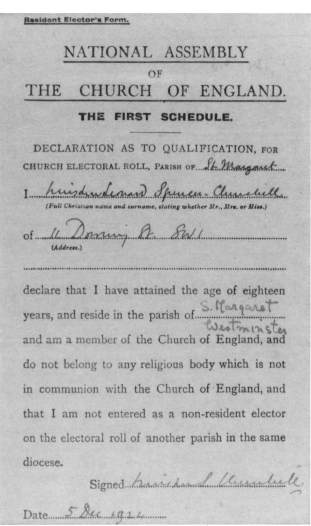

Stained glass window in memory of Speaker Fitzroy in St Margaret's Church (ABOVE)
Photo: B D R Fleming.

Application of Winston Churchill to join St Margaret's Parliamentary Parochial Roll, 5 December 1922 (ABOVE RIGHT)

of their number were elected to what was called 'the Parliamentary Church Council'. This Council took all the decisions necessary for running the Church and Parish.

The purpose of the Council was said to be threefold. In the first place, it was to give help and guidance on the needs and opportunities afforded by St Margaret's Church itself. Also it provided a forum where the Measures of the Church Assembly might be discussed. It was arranged that when a controversial issue was to be introduced, the details would be 'explained . . . by some competent member of the Assembly', and then his explanation discussed 'informally and privately'. The third purpose was more high-flown and idealistic.

> 'The council can promote a further purpose of far-reaching importance. In every department of contemporary life, and not least in the political province, we Christians find ourselves in the grip of un-Christian forces, not seldom actively anti-Christian. The ultimate problem which confronts us is that of arresting their onrush, and of maintaining the Christian basis of our civilisation: of securing the supremacy of Christian ideals and principles and standards of value. This problem will not be solved by the efforts of isolated individuals. Its menace must be met by the combined action of men who are able to give reasons for the faith that is in them, an ability which in these perplexing times can only be purchased at the cost of some clear thinking and

long-sighted anticipation. By providing a nucleus centre of intelligent and informed opinion the Council can help to create an atmosphere favourable to such efforts and thus make a contribution of great value to our healthy development as a Christian community'[51].

The procedure of electing a Parliamentary Church Council was continued at the beginning of each Parliament until 1963, when a Parochial Church Council, under the provisions of the *Representation of the Laity Measure 1956*, was formed. This council had six places reserved for Members of Parliament and the Speaker was a member *ex-officio*. It continued in this manner until the legal end of the Parish in 1973[52].

The Jurisdiction of the Dean and Chapter

Under the same piece of legislation that made the title 'Rector' honorific, there was also a change in the status of St Margaret's Church[53]. Since 1973 it has no longer been a Parish Church and the various parochial structures such as Parochial Church Councils no longer apply. All legal and financial responsibility now lies with the Dean and Chapter of Westminster.

Its previous parochial area in Westminster was divided between St Martin-in-the-Fields and St Matthew Westminster, but with the significant and important exception of the Palace of Westminster. This, like the Church and Churchyard of St Margaret's, was incorporated into the Parish of the Close of the Collegiate Church of St Peter Westminster and so the House of Commons is now situated ecclesiastically within that Close[54]. But, of course, that does not effect the association of the House with St Margaret's. Within the total jurisdiction of the Abbey exercised by the Dean and Chapter, it is recognised that this long-standing relationship will happily continue. When the Chapter of Westminster promoted the Bill, which was to give legal status to the changes, they saw to it that it contained this clause:

> 'Nothing in this Act shall effect the customary rights of the members and officers of either House of Parliament in relation to Saint Margaret's Church or Westminster Abbey'[55].

So it is that marriages of MPs and their children, baptisms and memorial services may still take place in what is now legally 'St Margaret's Church, Westminster Abbey'.

The use of the Chapel of St Mary Undercroft today

One apparent anomaly remains under the provisions of the 1972 Act. The only remnant of the building which contained the House of Commons' first permanent debating chamber – the Chapel of St Mary Undercroft – continues to be outside the jurisdiction of the Dean and Chapter of Westminster[56] and instead, as part of a Royal Palace, is under the supervision of the Lord Great Chamberlain who, by present custom, together with the Lord Chancellor and the Speaker of the House of Commons, regulates its use.

Earlier this century the matter of jurisdiction over the Chapel and the regulation of its use became a matter of some dissension. On 10 March 1924, J. I. Macpherson put down a question in the House of Commons for the First Commissioner of Works in which he asked:

> 'For what purposes the Crypt in the Royal Palace of Westminster has been used and under whose jurisdiction it is?'

John Austin Baker
Chaplain 1978–1982
HCCR

The Chapel of St Mary Undercroft during a special service.
Photo: Matthew Cummings Photography and National Asthma Campaign.

In his answer the Rt Hon. F. W. Jowett replied that the Chapel was 'under the general jurisdiction of the Lord Great Chamberlain' but that he, as First Commissioner of Works, was responsible for the fabric.

Mr Macpherson said that he found Jowett's answer unsatisfactory and gave notice that he intended to raise the matter at the Adjournment that night[57]. That evening Macpherson explained that he wished to have his son, David, baptised in the Chapel but that the Speaker's Chaplain (W. H. Carnegie) had refused to allow him to invite a Church of Scotland Minister to perform the ceremony. The Member challenged the Chaplain's ruling and said that he was asserting 'a pretended jurisdiction over the rights and privileges of the members of this House', and claimed that the Chapel was a Royal Peculiar exempted from the jurisdiction of the Ordinary. Jowett, in his response, agreed that the Chapel was not in a parish nor did it come under any ecclesiastical authority[58].

Two days later in *The Times* the Church of Scotland Minister (Revd Dr Archibald Fleming of St Columba's, Pont Street) who had been refused 'permission' to baptize Mr Macpherson's son, wrote to dispel any impression that 'Canon Carnegie's intransigence is typical of a more or less universal mood in the Church of England' and listed the many kindnesses and courtesies he had received at the hands of Anglican clergy 'from "high" churchmen as well as from "low" '. He finished by noting that from the First Commissioner's reply in the House it would appear that Carnegie's zeal had outrun his discretion.

The same edition of *The Times* also included a letter from Revd H. F. Westlake, Custodian and Minor Canon of Westminster and the historian of St Margaret's[59]. In his letter Westlake defended Carnegie's position. He reminded readers that during a quarrel over jurisdiction in 1398, between the Abbot of Westminster and the College of St Stephen, it was agreed that the Chapels of the Royal Palace should be outside abbatial control. Yet it was stated in the settlement that they were nonetheless *in parochia Sancte Margarete*. Westlake alleged that at the Dissolution the buildings would have reverted to parochial jurisdiction and as only the Chapel of St Stephen was given to the House of Commons by Edward VI:

> 'It may be supposed that such other portions of the old Palace as are occupied by members today are so occupied by right of user or by Royal courtesy. I think no right of user could be claimed in respect of the Chapel of St Mary'[60].

The discussion rumbled on for many months with the Archbishop of Canterbury (Randall Davidson) becoming involved.

Eventually it was agreed between the Speaker (J. H. Whitley), the Lord Great Chamberlain (the Marquess of Lincolnshire) and the King's Private Secretary (Lord Stamfordham) that the matter should be submitted by the Lord Great Chamberlain to the Law Officers of the Crown and that their judgement should be submitted to the Crown[61].

So when, over a year later, on 14 December 1925, Mr. Macpherson asked the Under Secretary of State for Home Affairs (Capt. D. H. Hacking), in another question in the House, if he would announce the Law Officers' decision regarding the jurisdiction over the Chapel, and to whom should application be made for permission to use the Chapel, he was told:

'The Law Officers decided that no ecclesiastical jurisdiction exists in respect of the Crypt Chapel. It is therefore under the sole jurisdiction of the Lord Great Chamberlain, to whom application should be made for permission to use the Chapel for baptisms, weddings etc. Arrangements in connection with the preparation of the Chapel for such ceremonies will be made by the Superintendent of Works'.

On hearing this, Macpherson triumphantly asked:

'May I take it from the answer that the Crypt of this ancient House is now available to Christians of all denominations?'

And the answer was:

'Certainly. Subject to the jurisdiction of the Lord Great Chamberlain'[62].

Thus the matter was settled and in such a manner it continues to be fully used. During Parliamentary sessions there is a weekly Church of England eucharist, but the rites of other Churches have been celebrated in the Chapel. It is here that many baptisms and weddings of those closely related to peers, members of the House of Commons and the officers of both Houses take place. As the marriage laws currently provide, only Church of England weddings can be solemnised, but Baptisms are performed by Priests and Ministers of various denominations. There are also other services in the Chapel, particularly Memorial Services. Although the Speaker's Chaplain has, from what has already been said, no proprietorial rights over the Chapel and its worship, he exercises, on behalf of the Lord Great Chamberlain and the others, a supervisory and advisory role in regard to the services which take place there.[63]

Christian fellowship in the Palace of Westminster

In 1956 the Speaker's Chaplain, Canon J. McLeod Campbell, encouraged the formation of the Houses of Parliament Christian Fellowship. The inaugural meeting was held on 21 November 1956, at which Mr Horace Holmes was elected the first Chairman.

It was intended that the meetings should be 'a Christian Fellowship of both Houses of Parliament and Staff'. By December of that year there was a total membership of 100, including some members of the Press Gallery. In the early meetings of the Fellowship there was much discussion as to whether there should be any definition of membership and also whether or not the Fellowship ought to be affiliated to any other organisation. It was eventually decided that a broad-based membership would be best and that a Christian Fellowship in the Palace of Westminster ought to be *sui generis* to avoid any political misunderstanding[64].

In more recent years staff members of the Fellowship have organised their own meetings with their own full programme under the general umbrella of the Parliamentary Christian Fellowship (which is the present title of the fellowship). There is also a lively Parliamentary Christian Wives group which meets weekly during the time that Parliament is sitting, as well as taking part in the other activities of the Fellowship.

John McLeod Campbell
Chaplain 1955–1961
HCCR

Breakfast in Speaker's House after the monthly Parliamentary Holy Communion in St Margaret's Church.
Photo: BBV TV, taken from the 'Songs of Praise' programme, transmitted 25 February 1990.

A Prayer Breakfast for Members, which consists of a celebration of the Holy Communion in St Margaret's Church followed by breakfast and a short address in Speaker's House, takes place each month except during parliamentary recesses.

The Fellowship continues to have a strong presence in the Palace of Westminster. The Rt Hon. Michael Alison MP, who was for a time its Chairman, has written:

> 'It is this aspect of Christianity, its capacity to unify men and women of goodwill, which makes it possible for MPs from every sort of party and denominational background to meet together in harmony and fellowship – as we regularly do in considerable numbers when Parliament is sitting – to share and deepen our insights into a common faith. The weekly study group, for example, which discusses the Old and New Testaments, often brings together an Ulster Unionist with a Roman Catholic, Anglican MPs of all sexes and parties, MPs of other denominations, and peers. They have no difficulty in praying together'[65].

It was in order to give permanence and continuity to all this activity that the Houses of Parliament Christian Fellowship Trust was launched in 1989. Speaking on that occasion, Michael Alison said:

> 'The Westminster Parliament is enormously privileged to enjoy a foundation and framework which expresses and sustains the Christian religion. But much of this heritage finds expression only in formal ritual; and without the sap of a living and active faith, the old forms could easily wither and decay.
>
> The Parliamentary Christian Fellowship exists to give life and vitality to what might otherwise turn to dry bones. It is very encouraging that well over 100 peers and MPs support some or all of the varied meetings and fixtures organised by the Fellowship, ranging from the quarterly buffet suppers, to the monthly breakfast with Mr. Speaker, and the weekly study groups'[66].

It is the hope of many, representing various aspects of Parliamentary life, that both the formal rituals and these other Christian activities will long have a significant place in the life of the Palace of Westminster.

Chapter Five

The Daily Prayers in the House of Commons

FROM 1558 UNTIL 1580 THE PRAYERS BEFORE THE commencement of the day's business consisted mainly of the saying of the Litany led by the Clerk of the House. From 1571 certainly, there was also a prayer said by the Speaker. The *Commons Journal* for 21 January 1581 records: 'The Litany being said by the Clerk and the old prayer that was used in former sessions read also by the Speaker'[1].

This might be said to be the beginning of 'Parliamentary Prayers' as such. The form of the Speaker's 'old prayer' which was in use in 1589 may well have been as follows:

> 'O Merciful God and Father, forasmuch as no counsel can stand, nor any can prosper, but such as are humbly gathered in Thy Name, to feel that sweet taste of Thy Holy Spirit, we gladly acknowledge that by Thy favour standeth the peaceable protection of our Queen and Realm, and likewise this favourable liberty granted unto us at this time to make our meeting together, which Thy bountiful goodness we most thankfully acknowledge, do withal earnestly pray Thy divine Majesty so to incline our hearts, as our counsel may be subject in true obedience to Thy Holy Word and Will. Andith it hath pleased Thee to govern this Realm by ordinary assembling the three estates of the same, our humble prayer is, that Thou wilt grant in us good minds to conceive, free liberty to speak, and on all sides a ready and quiet consent to such wholesome Laws and Statutes, as may declare us to be Thy people, and this Realm to be prosperously ruled by Thy good guiding and defence; so that we and our posterity may with cheerful hearts wait for Thy appearance in judgement, that art only able to present us faultless before God our heavenly Father to whom with Thee and our Saviour Christ and the Holy Spirit, be all glory both now and ever. Amen'[2].

It would seem that in the later Elizabethan Parliaments it became customary for the Speaker to use a prayer of his own composition. Speaker Yelverton in 1597 used a prayer which is recorded by D'Ewes:

> 'O Eternal God, Lord of Heaven and Earth, the great and mighty Counsellor, we, Thy poor servants assembled before Thee in this honourable senate, humbly acknowledge our great and manifold sins and imperfections, and thereby our unworthiness to receive any grace and assistance from Thee; yet, most merciful Father, since by Thy providence we are called from all parts of the land to this famous Council of Parliament to advise of those things which concern Thy glory, the good of Thy Church, the prosperity of our Prince, and the weal of her people: we most entirely beseech Thee that, pardoning all our sins in the blood of Thy Son Jesus Christ, it would please Thee, by the brightness of Thy Spirit, to expel darkness and vanity from our minds and partiality from our speeches, and grant unto us such wisdom and integrity of

**The Speakers Procession
1899**
Drawing by A Carruthers
Gould from *Lords and
Commons*, no. 1, 11 February
1899. It shows Speaker Gully
with his Chaplain, Basil
Wilberforce.

heart as becometh the servants of Jesus Christ, the subjects of a gracious Prince,
and members of this honourable House. Let not us, O Lord, who are met
together for the public good of the whole land, be more careless and remiss
than we use to be in our own private causes. Give grace, we beseech Thee, that
every one of us may labour to show a good conscience to Thy Majesty, a good
zeal to Thy Word, and a loyal heart to our Prince and a Christian love to our
country and commonwealth. O Lord, so unite and conjoin the hearts of her
excellent Majesty and this whole assembly as they may be a threefold cord not
easily broken: giving strength to such Godly laws as be already enacted, that
they may be better executed, and enacting such as are further requisite for the
bridling of the wicked, and the encouragement unto the Godly and well-
affected subjects, that so Thy great Blessing may be continued towards us, and
Thy grievous judgment turned from us. And that only for Christ Jesus sake,
our most glorious and only Mediator and Advocate, to whom with thy blessed
majesty and the Holy Ghost be given all Honour and Praise, Power and
Dominion from this time forth for evermore. Amen'[3].

Yelverton is said to have a 'flair for mellifluous prose'[4] and this he certainly
demonstrated in his prayer.

In the first Parliament of the reign of James I, the Clerk is recorded as reading 'such prayers as had been ordinary in former Parliaments in the reign of the late Queen'. Whether this was all, or part, of the Litany cannot be said with certainty. And once again 'one other special prayer, fitley conceived for that time and purpose' read by the Speaker. But the *Journal* in 1601 says that the addition of such a prayer was 'voluntary and not of Duty or Necessity, though hitherto, of late time, the like hath been done by other Speakers'. Speaker Phelips' prayer lacks some of the flair of his predecessor but one, and was far from brief:

'O God most great and glorious, which dwellest in the Heavens over all, yet humblest thyself to behold the Things that are done upon the Earth; we thy People, and Sheep of thy Pasture, assembled, by thy Providence, to the Performance of this high Service, whereupon the Honour of thy Name, the Beauty of thy Church amongst us, the Glory of our King, and Wealth of our State, doth depend; knowing, that without thee we can do nothing, do at this Time, with Fear and Reverence, in the Beginning of our Consultations, first look up to thee, from whom Wisdom and happy Success doth come; praying thee to look down from Heaven upon us with the Eye of thy Mercy; to draw near unto us with the Presence of thy Grace; to prepare us all with Counsel and Understanding; and to be President and Director of all our Conferences; that those things may be propounded, conceived, allowed, and confirmed, that may best please thee, and most directly and soundly uphold the Honour of thy Name, the Sincerity of thy Worship, the Safety of our King, and Peace of thy People, even for thy Son our Lord's sake. And that we may not ourselves be any Lett to the Obtaining of these our Desires, either by means of any Sin formerly committed, or of any Corruption yet remaining in us; we humbly pray thee to forgive our Sins, and to blot out all our Iniquities; and to stand reconciled unto us in an everlasting Covenant of Peace, as if we had never sinned against thee. And because our Hearts, by Nature, are not fit for good Cogitations, create a new Heart, and renew a right Spirit, in us; remove far from us all vain-glorious Humour of commending our own Wit, all covetous Humour of advancing our private Profit, all envious Humour of disgracing other Mens Gifts, all malicious Humour of hurting any Man's Person, and finally, all froward Humour of opposing ourselves against just, needful, and godly things, by whomsoever propounded. Furnish us with Knowledge, Wisdom and Zeal, by sending down thy Spirit into our Hearts, that we may understand, discern, prefer, and set forward, all things tending to the Advancement of thy Glory, and such as may be thought worthy of our Assent and Furtherance.
And because all good things are not of equal Goodness, nor all needful things of equal Necessity; let our Care and Zeal be equally proportioned to the Degrees of Things, in Goodness and Necessity different: And therefore, first, make us careful of the Glory of thy Name, which is the high End of all thy Counsels and Works, and ought to be the last End, but first respected, of all our Purposes and Doings; and therein let our special religious Practice of thy Worship, by the Ministry and Means that Christ hath planted in his Church: Next, let the Good of this whole Island move our Care and Zeal; which consisting in the Safety and Honour of the King, and the Enacting and Executing of good Laws, let us be wisely careful, and faithfully zealous for the Person of our King, whom thou, the King of Kings, hast in Mercy set over us. And because no Law can be good that is not agreeable to thy Law, which containeth the fundamental Equity of our Laws in making Laws to govern thy People, let us always have an Eye unto thy Law, not digressing from the holy Equity thereof; and what through thy Mercy we shall here profitably enact, we

Arthur Onslow (ABOVE)
Chaplain 1774–1779
Photo: reproduced from an
engraving in Worcester
Cathedral Library by kind
permission of the Dean and
Chapter of Worcester.

Henry White (ABOVE RIGHT)
**Chaplain 1869–1874 and
1889–1890**
'Not having been passed
through one of the ancient
Universities Mr White has
been looked upon by his
clerical brethren as an
unwarranted interloper in the
fields of patronage.
Nevertheless he has had some
successes in the pastures which
are fenced off against
trespassers. His facile sermons
are only five-and-twenty
minutes long, and he is a
"Royal Peculiar".' (*Vanity
Fair*, 26 December 1874)

pray thee, through the whole Kingdom it may be truly executed, that our great
Labour may not be disgraced with little Fruit.

Here us, we pray thee, O Father of Mercy, in these our most humble and
needful Petitions; forgive, and answer us, according to thy fatherly and great
Goodness, for Jhesus Christ his Sake; to whom, with thee and the Holy Ghost,
Three Persons and One God, be all Praise, Glory and Power, now and for
ever'[5].

For a while it would seem that 'Mr. Speaker's Prayer' could be said by the
Clerk. On 11 February 1605 it is recorded:

'The ordinary Prayers and Mr. Speaker's Prayer read by the Clerk, Mr. Speaker
waiting upon the King till after Nine a'clock'[6].

But in 1606 it was clearly laid down that only the Speaker should perform that
part of the devotions:

'Prayers were said by the Clerk, but not the Prayer wonted to be said by Mr.
Speaker; being so directed by the House'[7].

On the Restoration in 1660, a committee was appointed to 'inform themselves
as to what form of prayer had hitherto been used in the House'[8], but there is
no record of any report of their findings having been made by the Committee
to the House. Similarly, Sir B. Hicks asked permission in 1624 to introduce 'a

Prayer of Thanksgiving' to be said at the Parting of Parliament, but this also was never done[9].

It is generally asserted that the prayers at present in daily use in the House date from the Restoration. From the content of them it is obvious that they could have had no origin in anything that would have been prayed in the Parliament which met between 1649 and 1660.

An examination of the Prayers[10]

The prayers start with the Chaplain reciting Psalm 67 (*Deus Misereatur*), without doxology, in a translation which is the work of Coverdale in *The Great Bible* of 1539. The Chaplain then greets the members with 'The Lord be with you', to which they reply before he says, 'Let us pray'. This is the signal for a singular custom. The Members now turn inwards, that is, with their backs to the Speaker and the Chaplain, and face their seats and they remain thus for the rest of the prayers. This seems to be a modification of a previous custom in which members turned and knelt on their seats which provided a more practical height at which to kneel when wearing a sword. In the House of Lords many of their lordships still kneel on the benches in this manner.

Samuel Smith
Chaplain 1802–1806
Photo: from a portrait by Joseph Bouet, by kind permission of the Durham University Library (NSR.7.D.6).

There follows the three-fold *Kyrie* and then the Lord's Prayer. The version used follows closely Tyndale's translation of 1526 for the first part, but the conclusion 'for thine is the Kingdom . . . ' is first found in the *Scottish Book of Common Prayer* of 1637[11].

The prayer for the Sovereign which follows next has a long and complicated history. The first version of it appeared 'officially' in the *Primer* of 1553 but is clearly derived from a prayer by John Fisher in his *Psalmi seu precationes* (1525) translated by T. Berthelet in 1544 under the title *Psalmes or Prayers taken out of holie Scripture*[12].

The next prayer is one for the Royal Family. There was no Prayer for the Royal Family in any Prayer Book until 1662. The precedent of praying for members of the Royal Family was set when a limited number of them were mentioned in the Litany of 1544. The present prayer is based on one which was first used around 1604. At that time it was to be used in worship after the Litany proper had been completed[13]. There is an early copy of this prayer in the Westminster Abbey Muniments dating from 1611. This prayer has often been modified as births and deaths in the Royal Family have necessitated[14].

The provenance of the Prayer for Parliament, which now follows, has been a matter of some debate. It is certainly 'the centre-piece' of the short daily service. One version of its origin is given by Lord Hemingford, although the historicity of his story is extremely doubtful:

> 'A curious story is told as to the origin and authorship of this prayer which has been in use for many years, not only in the House of Commons but also in the House of Lords, where prayers in the same form are said by one of the Bishops. A Select Committee, it is said, was set up to consider and settle the form of the prayers to be said at the commencement of each day's sittings: the Committee

Speaker Fitzroy, with his Chaplain, Alan Don, outside Speaker's House before leaving for the Coronation in Westminster Abbey, 12 May 1937.
HCCR

decided on the 67th Psalm, the Lord's Prayer, the Prayers for the Sovereign and the Royal Family and so on: but they desired to include a prayer specially appropriate for use by Parliament, asking God's blessing upon their work for the nation; they asked the Chairman of the Committee to compose such a prayer for their consideration: he gave much anxious attention to this task without settling anything to his satisfaction: but one night he retired to bed after thinking much on the matter and dreamed a dream: he dreamt that an Angel woke him and told him to get up and write what he (the Angel) should dictate, and then dictated this prayer: the Chairmen met his committee the following day, told them of his dream, said he thought the prayer was a perfect one, but that unfortunately he could not remember it! He promised to go home and to try his hardest to recollect it: on returning to his house and going into his room, he found lying there a sheet of paper on which in his own handwriting was the prayer which the Angel had dictated, and which he must have written down at the Angel's dictation, in his sleep; he submitted it to his Committee who approved and adopted it without alteration as divinely inspired. The story may be a curious one, but it is far from absurd: it is well known in these days, that the brain may continue working during sleep with the result that a 'dream' may solve a problem which the sleeper has been thinking about'[15].

We have noted the prayers used in 1580, 1597 and 1603[16] and although they have certain affinities to the prayer as now used, it also has a resemblance to the prayer for the High Court of Parliament which was included in the Book of Common Prayer in 1662, the authorisation of which was an almost contemporary event. That prayer is reputed to have been composed by William Laud, when he was Bishop of St David's, for the service on a special fast day in 1625[17]. But it is certainly not the work of Speaker Yelverton as has sometimes been asserted[18].

The last prayer, 'Prevent us, O Lord', is a translation of a collect *Actiones nostras quesumus domine* which is in *Sacramentarium Gregorianum* and is 'clearly derived from an older prayer in the Gelasian Sacramentary'[19]. This collect appeared in the Book of Common Prayer of 1549 where it was included among six collects to be said after the offertory, when there is no communion[20]. It is usual to ascribe the authorship of the translations of ancient collects which are contained in the 1549 book to Cranmer and this may well be true. However, we must not forget that although Cranmer was chiefly responsible for the 1549 book (perhaps less so for the Prayer Book of 1552), he did have the assistance of twelve colleagues, six bishops and six learned divines in the compilation of the book. Liturgical Commissions are not a twentieth century invention[21].

'The Grace' (2 Cor. 13.14) was first added as a conclusion to a service in 'The Litany used in the Queen's Chapel' of 1559 and thence found its way into the Elizabethan Prayer Book[22]. Until 1983 the Grace had always been said by the Chaplain alone, but since then the Speaker and the Members have joined him in the saying of this final prayer.

The Absence of the Chaplain

It is well established that if the Chaplain is absent from prayers (and he has not provided a deputy to act for him) this does not mean that the laudable custom of the House of Commons commencing its proceedings with its customary devotions needs to be omitted. On these occasions the custom is that the Speaker conducts the prayers himself. The even older custom of the Clerk of the House saying the Prayers[23] is not now possible, because the Clerk does not enter the House until after Prayers have been completed[24].

Prayer Cards

There is a Parliamentary custom associated with Prayers which must be mentioned. It concerns what are known as 'Prayer Cards'. The convention is that a seat in the Chamber which has been marked by the placing by a Member of one of these cards before the commencement of business is reserved for the use of that member for the rest of the parliamentary day. However, the validity of such a reservation depends entirely upon the fact that the Member is actually occupying the seat during Prayers[25]. This was established as long ago as 26 November 1640 when it was resolved:

> 'that neither book nor glove may give any man title or interest to any place, if they themselves be not at prayers'[26].

House of Commons Prayer Card, as in current use.

Variations in the Prayers

The daily prayers have remained unchanged since the seventeenth century, with the only additions and subtractions being the necessary alterations in the name of the Sovereign and members of the Royal Family. These would be done according to the Royal Warrants issued from time to time to procure those same alterations in the Book of Common Prayer[27].

The prayers in the House of Lords[28] follow the same pattern as those in the Commons except that in recent times the Bishop who conducts the prayers in that House has had a choice of Psalms with which to commence the act of worship rather than the unchanging Psalm 67[29]. When the Lords made this change in 1970 there was some discussion as to whether the Speaker's Chaplain ought to be given a similar discretion over the opening Psalm, but it was decided not to make any change[30].

There are only two recorded examples of deviations from the norm, both in the twentieth century. The first came on 26 October 1950 when the rebuilt House of Commons Chamber, which had been erected on the same site and in the same 'Collegiate' style as the one which had been destroyed by enemy action, was officially opened. There were two innovations at Prayers that day: first, there were present a large number of the Speakers from other legislatures of the Commonwealth[31]. Secondly, after the Chaplain (Prebendary Cheshire) had said the normal, traditional prayers, the Dean of Westminster,

Christopher Cheshire Chaplain 1946–1955
HCCR

Dr A. C. Don (who had himself been Speaker's Chaplain throughout the war years), added a special prayer for the occasion:

'O God, the Judge of all the earth, who has been our refuge and strength from one generation to another, we humbly seek Thy blessing.

We praise Thee for the powers of mind and skill of hand that have gone to the building of this Chamber, and for the generosity of many peoples in diverse lands whose gifts have beautified and enriched it.

We thank Thee for the goodly heritage bequeathed to us by those who in times past have served Thee in this place, and we pray that entering into their labour we may be found worthy guardians of the honour of this House.

Guide and control, we beseech Thee, our deliberations, making us so mindful of our trust that truth and righteousness, justice and liberty may ever flourish and abound, and the people of this Realm may find their perfect freedom in Thy service. And grant, that as we seek to know Thy will we may have patience to fulfil it, to Thy glory and the good of all mankind.

Hear us, O merciful Father, in heaven Thy dwelling place and when Thou hearest, forgive; for the sake of Him who is the only sure foundation of men and nations, Jesus Christ our Lord. Amen[32]'.

Alan Don (BELOW LEFT)
Chaplain 1936–1946
HCCR

Trevor Beeson (BELOW RIGHT)
Chaplain 1982–1987
HCCR

Alan C. Don — Chaplain to the Speaker. 1936–1946

T S Nevill
Chaplain 1969–1972
HCCR

After Prayers the Speaker said:

> 'I should explain that normally no one is admitted to the Galleries until we have finished our daily Prayers. They may well be called our family Prayers. But it is fitting on this unique occasion, seeing that we all belong to one great family of nations, that our Prayers this morning should be witnessed and shared by representatives from every part of our great Commonwealth family'.

Mr. Speaker Clifton-Brown concluded his speech by saying:

> 'Finally, may I, as your Speaker, welcome all my fellow Members back to their old home ... Our first act on coming home has been one of worship and of dedication and in all humbleness of heart I pray "May the Almighty God bless our home" '[33].

The second occasion when there was a variation was on 22 June 1965 on the occasion of the seventh centenary of Simon de Montfort's Parliament. That day there were to be special ceremonies, but before the two Houses assembled in Westminster Hall for these, they each held prayers in their own Chamber. The form of prayer was as usual except that before the final collect 'Prevent us, O Lord' the following prayer was used:

> 'Almighty and Eternal God, Thou Judge of all the earth, Who hast been our refuge from one generation to another, we humbly seek Thy blessing as we meet to commemorate the Seven Hundredth Anniversary of the Parliament of Simon de Montfort.
> We praise thy name, O Lord, for the goodly heritage bequeathed to us by those who, in bygone days, have served Thee here and for the guidance of Thy Spirit throughout the ages.
> Especially do we thank Thee for that thou didst inspire the minds of our Rulers in times past to call into consultation those representatives of the Shires, Cities and Boroughs of England who, in due time, were to constitute the House of Commons.
> Grant that in this place truth and justice, liberty and righteousness may ever flourish and abound, and that, as we seek to know Thy will, we may have strength and power to fulfil it to the glory of Thy Holy Name and the good of all mankind.
> All this we ask for the sake of Him, who is the only sure foundation of men and of nations, even Jesus Christ, Our Lord. Amen'[34].

The prayer was said by the Acting Chaplain, Revd T. S. Nevill, in the absence of Canon Stancliffe[35].

As on the previous occasion 'strangers contrary to the normal practice, were allowed to occupy seats in the galleries while the prayers were said'[36].

A clergyman in his outdoor dress from an 18th century print. Note his cassock, gown and chapeau.
'Lusus Naturæ, or Carracaturas of the Present Age'. Published March 5th 1752. Sold by B Dickenson on Ludgate Hill in George Paston, *Social Caricatures in the Eighteenth Century*, New York, 1968.

The Speaker's Procession and the Prayers – present practice

The Chaplain enters the chamber to conduct prayers as part of the Speaker's Procession[37]. He has dressed in the traditional robes in his room to which there is an entrance in Lower Library Corridor, although the room itself is actually part of Speaker's House[38]. These robes consist of a black silk cassock which needs to be 'not too long to cover his black silk stockings and court shoes with silver buckles'[39]. To this is added white linen bands. Over the cassock is worn what Thorne describes as 'a black silk Geneva gown', but it would seem that this is more accurately the Priest's gown of the normal outdoor habit of a clergyman. This form of dress (including the gown) is said

Donald Gray (ABOVE LEFT)
Chaplain 1987–
HCCR

**Badge on the scarf, or
tippet, which the Speaker's
Chaplain wears each day at
Prayers** (ABOVE RIGHT)

to have survived until about 1810 and then was used only as the correct dress for the clergy when at Court, which would explain its retention in this context[40].

The Chaplain wears a scarf (or tippet) which is embroidered at each end with the Royal Arms, surmounted by a crown, and the words 'House of Commons'. He wears white gloves, and carries a black three-cornered hat, called a chapeau[41], and a handkerchief. The latter, surely, a relic of the scented handkerchief which was necessary in those days when, even within the Palace of Westminster, the smell of the Thames would be overpowering to delicate nostrils.

After processing through the corridors the Chaplain enters the Chamber together with the Speaker, the Serjeant at Arms and the Speaker's Secretary. They bow together at the Bar of the House towards the Chair. It is fitting that the ceremony of prayers should so commence, because the custom of 'bowing to the chair' derives from the fact that when the Members of the Commons took over the Collegiate Church of St Stephen in 1547 the Speaker's Chair was placed in front of the Altar and the members of the House, churchmen all, knew from their youngest days that the respect due to an altar in any church was a solemn bow[42].

When they have bowed, the Serjeant, the Speaker and the Chaplain advance seven paces before bowing again. Meanwhile the Speaker's Secretary has left the Chamber. During prayers the Serjeant and the Chaplain are the only non-members present. All the other officers and staff do not enter the Chamber until after prayers; the public and press galleries are not open until

The Speaker's Procession at the State Opening of Parliament, 7 November 1990.
Left to right: J Town, Bar Doorkeeper; Sir Alan Urwick, KCVO, CMG, Serjeant at Arms; the Rt Hon. Bernard Weatherill MP, Speaker; D J Lord, Trainbearer; P J Kitcatt, CB, Speaker's Secretary; Canon D C Gray TD, Speaker's Chaplain.

the daily devotions of the House have been completed[43]. The private nature of prayers was re-emphasised by Mr Speaker Weatherill in a reply to a point of order in October 1989 which asked for assurance that in no circumstances would prayers ever be televised. This was just before the commencement of the televising of the Commons debates. He said, 'I confirm that Prayers have always been and will remain private'[44].

After the second bow, the Serjeant places the Mace on the table and the Speaker and the Chaplain move to places which are side by side at the Table below the Speaker's chair. When at the words 'Let us pray', as previously noted[45], the Members turn to face their seats, the Speaker and the Chaplain kneel at special stools which are provided.

After prayers there are a further series of bows, before the Chaplain leaves the Chamber, being careful to cross over the Bar of the House walking backwards. Having completed this hazardous operation he bows for the last time before leaving the Chamber and walks directly into Member's Lobby for an almost inevitable 'lobbying' by some member or other who has a question or query either trivial or grave which he or she wishes the Chaplain to deal with. The Chaplain is still working and exercising his ministry to the House long after he has finished saying the daily prayers in the Chamber.

Part Two

Introduction

A biographical listing of Chaplains in
chronological order from 1660 to 1991

**'The House of Commons at
Prayer.'**
From a drawing in the
Speaker's Chaplain's Room
by A Castaigne, dated 1903.

Francis Gastrell
Chaplain 1702–1704
Photo: reproduced from a
portrait in Bishop's House,
Chester by kind permission of
the Lord Bishop of Chester
and the Church
Commissioners for England.

Introduction

ALTHOUGH AT FIRST SIGHT THE FOLLOWING 'POTTED biographies' of those who have held the office of Chaplain to the Speaker of the House of Commons may seem to have a disappointing sameness about them, only a little searching below the surface of the details of academic achievement and ecclesiastical preferments has revealed priests of varying talents and abilities, as well as men of diverse virtues; and no doubt, despite the high calling of their profession, varying defects.

As already has been noted, up to 1835 a clear career pattern is not only discernable, but it was also confidently expected by the office-holder. Although the guarantee of further preferment has now been removed it remains a fact that many of those who have been Speaker's Chaplain have gone on to serve the Church (and Nation) with continuing distinction in other spheres. However, in the days of promised promotion, it is not surprising to learn that it was not always the undisputed opinion of other churchmen that particular Speaker's Chaplains were deserving of the advancement that became their prerogative. Of William Galloway (1698) it was said that he was 'a most notorious stupid blockhead, without a grain of learning, (who) for being Foley's Chaplain when Speaker, got to be Prebendary of Worcester; which to the scandel of all worthy men he still enjoys'[1].

In contrast, Frances Gastrell (1702), who went on to become Bishop of Chester, made a better impression on his contemporaries and prompted Samuel Wesley (brother of John and Charles) to write of him on his death:

> 'I sing of a Prelate good, unbodied now,
> Nor longer Angel of the Church below;
> Enthron'd Triumphant! May the lines be free
> From sordid hope, and service flattery.
> Such views, if known, this happy Saint would move
> To shake his radiant head, and frown above'[2].

There were others, in the succession which follows, who sought to guarantee their earthly (if not necessarily their heavenly) rewards by other means than mere reliance on ecclesiastical and political favours. Peter Birch (1689), whose father had been a prominent member of the Parliamentary Army, not only became very respectably Church of England but was also careful to explore other reliable avenues to material comfort. It is recorded that 'he is a forward, illiterate man, but has had good luck by rich wives'[3]. Relationships of various degrees provided other means of insurance against being forgotten by the uncertain processes of patronage and preferment. Nepotism, for instance, appears to have been rife. Henry Carpenter (1662) was the uncle of Edward Turnor, Speaker 1661–71; whereas Thomas Goddard (1705) was appointed by his uncle (John Smith); as was Richard Cope (1751), his uncle being Richard Onslow. Arthur Onslow (1774), was also a nephew of Speaker Onslow, but he was appointed to the post by Speaker Norton. Folliott Cornewall (1780) was also distantly related to Onslow but owed his appointment to 'the interest of his second cousin Speaker Cornwall[4]. Speaker Manners-Sutton provided three members of his family as his Chaplains during various periods of his long occupancy of the Chair (1817–1835): Thomas Manners Sutton (1824), Evelyn Levett Sutton (1827) and Frederick Vernon Lockwood (1830). There is one example of father and son both occupying the office: Thomas Manningham (1690) and his son, also Thomas, in 1719. The elder Manningham was dismissed by Hearne as a 'bombast writer'[5].

Not surprisingly, allowing for the period in which they served, both Barton (1695) and Hallifax (1698) were 'puritanically inclined'. Barton was reckoned to be 'a pretty good scholar but a man of morose severe temper'[6]. Hallifax (1698) was also a scholar and did archeological work in Smyrna, copying out inscriptions at Palmyra, but was equally 'of the same puritanical stamp'[7] with Barton.

Another of the clerical scandals of the eighteenth and early nineteenth centuries is clearly demonstrated in the biographies of the Speaker's Chaplains of that period. They were almost all pluralists. That is, they held more than one cure of souls simultaneously. Sometimes the benefices were miles apart and there was little chance of anything more than an occasional visit to the parish in which the incumbent was non-resident[8]. From his often not inconsiderable means the pluralist engaged a curate to whom he paid a pittance[9]. Then, to what he derived from his benefices, the well-placed and well-connected clergyman could also add the benefits from a Cathedral or Collegiate prebend[10].

There was also the possibility that, having obtained a prebend, the priest could further add to his income by arranging that he was presented to one of the parishes (preferably a wealthy one) within the gift of the Chapter to which he now belonged. So, for example, Richard Cope (1751) was Rector of Islip as well as a Prebendary of Westminster; Islip is an Abbey living[11]. Thomas Causton (1795) was also Rector of Turweston (in the gift of the Westminster Chapter) as well as enjoying his prebend[12], and Laurence Broderick (1708) managed, at various times, to be Rector of both Islip and Turweston in addition to being a Prebendary of Westminster[13]. Reeve Ballard (1754) added St Bride's Fleet Street (also an Abbey living) to his income[14]. Of the Chaplains who went to be Canons of Christ Church, Oxford there is a splendid example of an attempt at bi-location in Frederick Barnes (1806) who managed for nearly fifty years to combine his duties in Oxford with those of being the Vicar of Colyton in Devon[15].

Further examples abound and can be easily discerned in their biographies. Scawen Kendrick (1729) who was for thirty-one years Rector of Hambleden, and died there, was also Archdeacon of Westminster, Sub Dean of Westminster and Rector of St Margaret's[16]; Philip Williams (1784), who combined the tasks of being Rector of Compton in Hampshire with those of being Rector of Gosberton in Lincolnshire, did this as well as being a Prebendary at Winchester[17].

Yet the most outrageous example of the misuse of ecclesiastical patronage in the following entries must be that of Charles Moss (1789). He was given the Sub-Deanery of Wells by his father, who was Bishop of Bath and Wells, in 1774. At that time Charles was aged 11[18].

Although it would seem that it was not until as late as 1880 that Disraeli

Charles Moss (ABOVE LEFT)
Chaplain 1789–1791
Photo: reproduced from a portrait at 1 Millbank by kind permission of the Lord Bishop of Oxford and the Church Commissioners for England.

Charles Merivale (ABOVE RIGHT)
Chaplain 1863–1869
HCCR

coined the phrase 'muscular christianity'[19], he would have recognised that particular combination of virtues in at least two of the Speaker's Chaplains who served the House during his own Parliamentary career. Charles Merivale (1863) had played for Harrow in the cricket match against Eton in 1824. On that occasion the Captain of the team had been Charles Wordsworth (whose father, to add to the coincidence, had been Speaker's Chaplain in 1818). Wordsworth went up to Christ Church, Oxford, while Merivale went to St John's at Cambridge[20]. It is acknowledged that it was out of the friendship of these two undergraduates that came the idea of the first University Boat Race:

> 'Encouraged by the example of the inter-University cricket match, which had taken place in 1827, we talked over the possibility of getting up a similar competition in rowing'[21].

Even so, that was not the full extent of the reach of the long arm of coincidence. The Oxford boat, which had Wordsworth rowing at four, had a Thomas Garnier of Worcester College at six[22]. Garnier was to be Speaker's Chaplain between 1849 and 1857. Thus, with Merivale in the Cambridge boat and Garnier in the dark blues boat, the first Boat Race in 1829 had a man destined to perform that same parliamentary rôle in each of the boats.

The only other sportsman among the Chaplains, of which there is evidence, is John Vane (1835) who had the reputation of being one of the best fighters of his time at Westminster School[23]. But many believe that the concept of muscular christianity attained its fictional apotheosis in the book entitled *Eric or Little by Little*[24] which was written by Frederick Farrar (Chaplain 1890), who also attained posthumous fame by being the maternal grandfather of Field Marshal Bernard Montgomery[25]. However, there was much more to Farrar than either of these facts reveal[26].

Many of the Chaplains came from aristocratic stock, two becoming peers.

Francis Byng
Chaplain 1874–1889
HCCR

George Ingram succeeding to the title of Viscount Irwin in 1761 and Frances Byng having to actually resign from office on becoming the 5th Earl of Stafford in 1899, after 15 years service in the House of Commons. John Vane (1835) was the natural son of the 1st Duke of Cleveland, whereas it was believed that William Burchett came from an entirely different background. Tradition has it that his father was Josiah Burchett, body servant of Pepys, who nevertheless himself became Secretary to the Admiralty and Member of Parliament for Sandwich (1721–41)[27]. Many were 'sons of the cloth', three of a cloth that was destined to become purple in later life[28]. Christopher Wordsworth, Chaplain 1818, was the brother of the poet William Wordsworth and part of a family that provided many distinguished clergyman.

Two of the Chaplains had close connections with great parliamentary names of the nineteenth century. Basil Wilberforce (1896) was grandson of William Wilberforce the Emancipator, and W. H. Carnegie (1916) married the widow of Joseph Chamberlain, who was a pillar of the Commons for thirty-eight years[29].

If this was not a work of historical accuracy it might have been possible to leave one scandalous clerical skeleton safely locked in the Chaplaincy cupboard. But it is, so it isn't.

We have already noted that Thomas Goddard was appointed Chaplain by his uncle Speaker Smith in 1705. He had come down from Oxford in 1689, thankfully with a degree, because:

> 'when he was of Magd. Col. in Oxon was commonly call'd *Honest Tom Goddard* because of his being a true friend to *Pot & Pipe*, and was a good natur'd Rake'[30].

It was a reputation that Goddard took with him in his performance of his duties in the Commons. Hearne records that his inclination to be 'a good natur'd Rake' was:

> 'a character which suits very well with him still, it being observ'd that the very first time he read Prayers after being made Chaplain he read the Evening for the Morning Service, having drunk to excess the night before that his head was giddy when he should perform his duty ye day after'[31].

As far as we know, Goddard died peacefully at Bath in his sixtieth year, whereas Evelyn Levett Sutton's demise in 1835 was nothing if not dramatic. He died suddenly 'attacked with apoplexy while reading the ninth commandment' in Westminster Abbey[32]!

Biographies of Speakers Chaplains 1660–1991

NOTE *Between 1675 and 1736 the exact date of the appointment of the Chaplain is not always known. Often the first mention of the Chaplain's name is in the address which the House made to the sovereign for some ecclesiastical preferment to be bestowed upon their chaplain as a token of their appreciation of his services. Thus the convention of using the phrase "by [year]" has been used to indicate the date by which there is certain knowledge of him being in service.*

1 1660 VOYCE (or VOICE) Edward
Appointed by Speaker Grimston. Address 6 Sept. 1660
Son of Edward Voyce Rector of West Stow
Born ? 1633   *Died* 1712
Education: Bury St Edmunds, Matric. Sizar from Corpus Christi Cambridge Easter 1651, Migrated to Emmanuel 1652
BA 1645   MA 1658
p. 1658
Rector of Oakley, Suffolk 1661–1712, Vicar of Hindolveston, Norfolk 1662–3, Rector of Twyford 1662–1671

CJ, viii, 155; *ibid.*, 229; *Al. Cant. (1)*, iv, 306; Tanner, *Norwich Bishop's Registers*, REG 19, book 26

2 1662 CARPENTER, Henry
Appointed by Speaker Turnor. Address 18 March 1662
Son of the Revd Richard Carpenter of Cullompton Devon
Born 1606 at Cullompton   *Died* 14 Oct. 1662 (buried at St Dionis Backchurch)
Education: Matric. Exeter Oxford 1624
BA 1628   BA (Cantab) incorporated 1632   DD 1662
Vicar of Holy Trinity Coventry 1663–6, Rector of Gretford, Lincs. 1635–6, Vicar of Steeple Ashton, Wilts. 1636–60, Vicar of Hilperton, Wilts. 1638–62, Rector of St Dionis, Backchurch, London 1661–2, Prebendary of Yetminster Prima in Salisbury Cathedral 1660, Rector of Stapleford Tawney, Essex 1661–2, Canon of Windsor, appointed 20 May 1662

CJ, viii, 388; *Al. Cant. (1)*, i, 294; *Al. Oxon. (1)*, i, 239; *Fasti. Wynd.*, 112, FES, ii, 435; *Rep. Eccl.*, i, 331; *Nov. Rep.*, 81 & LVIII

3 1663 WOTTON, Henry

Appointed by Speaker Turnor. Address 17 July 1663
Born ?
Died ? (buried 8 March 1709 at Little Parndon)
Education: Magdalen Oxford
MA 1649
Fellow of Magdalen 1648 (appointed by the Visitors)
Rector of Little Parndon, Essex, (Turnor's home) 1660,
Canon of Windsor, installed 28 May 1669, resigned 1 May 1671

CJ, viii, 525; *ibid.*, 643; *Fasti Wynd.*, 77; *Al. Oxon. (1)*, iv, 1683; Montague Burrows,
Register of the Visitors of the University of Oxford 1647–58, Camden Society 1881, 519;
History of Harlow, 1969, 81; *Essex Records Office, Little Parndon Registers*, D/P 34/1/2.

4 by 1675 BARKER, Joseph

Appointed by Speaker Seymour. Address 13 Nov. 1675
Born ?   Died ? 1698
Rector of Buckland St Mary, Somerset, Chaplain to Dowager Duchess
of Somerset 1660, Rector of Shipton Beauchamp 1661–98, Prebendary
of Wells (by 1676)

CJ, ix, 375; *CSPD* (1675–6), 167; *ibid.*, (1676–7), 264; *VCH Somerset*, iv, 218n, 219;
Nobleman's Register, Lambeth; Cant. Acts, iv, 79

5 by 1689 WILLET, Ralph

Appointed by Speaker Powle. Addresses 20 Aug. 1689, 19 May 1690
Born ? 1656   *Died* 20 Aug. 1738 (buried and monument at Stratton)
Education: Matric. St John's Oxford 1672, Scholar Wadham 1675
BA 1676   MA 1678   MA (Cantab) incorporated 1680
Fellow of Wadham 1678
Rector of Stratton, Glos. 1685–1717, Rector of Minchinhampton with
Rodburgh 1717–20, Rector of Tetbury, Glos. 1727–8, Rector of
Rodmarton, Glos. 1731–4, Rector of Great Wishford, Wilts. 1734–8,
Rural Dean of Cirencester.

CJ, x, 270; *ibid.*, 420; *Al. Cant. (1)*, i, 413; *Al. Oxon. (1)*, iv, 1636; *Cant. Acts*, viii, 17;
Parish Records Stratton;

6 by 1689 BIRCH, Peter

Appointed by Speaker Powle? (No addresses)
Son of Thomas Birch of Birch Hall Manchester (Colonel in
Parliamentary Army, MP for Liverpool)
Born ? 1652   *Died* 2 July 1710 (buried in Westminster Abbey)
Education: Matric. Christ Church Oxford 1673
BA 1674   MA 1674   BD 1684   DD 1688
Chaplain and Minor Canon Christ Church, Curate of St Thomas
Oxford, Rector of St Ebbe's, Lecturer at Carfax, Chaplain to James,
Duke of Ormond, Prebendary of Westminster, installed 17 Oct. 1689,
Sub Dean and Archdeacon, Rector of St James, Westminster 1692–4,
Vicar of St Bride's Fleet Street 1694–1710

WAR, 268; *Al. Oxon. (1)*, i, 126; *Hearne*, i, 106, 231; *Luttrell*, ii, 45, 520; *ibid.*, iii, 426;
ibid., iv, 284, *ibid.*, v, 251, *ibid.*, vi, 601; *Athenae*, iv, 659; *Fasti Ox.*, i, 334, 404; *Nov.
Rep.*, 113, 250, 448; *Rep. Eccl.*, i, 317, 661, 922

7 by 1690 MANNINGHAM, Thomas
Appointed by Speaker Trevor. Addresses 23 May 1690, 3 Jan. 1691,
19 Dec. 1691, 8 Dec. 1692.
Son of Richard Manningham, Rector of Michelmersh, Hants.
Born ? 1651 *Died* 25 Aug. 1772 (buried in St Andrew's Holborn)
Education: Winchester, Scholar of New Oxford 1669.
BA 1673 MA 1677 DD (Lambeth) 1691
Fellow of New College 1671–81.
Rector of East Tisted, Hants. 1681,
Preacher at the Rolls 1684, Headmaster Westerham G.S. 1689–92,
Rector of St Andrew Holborn 1691–1712, Canon of Windsor, installed
28 Jan. 1693, Rector of Great Hasley, Oxford 1708, Dean of Windsor,
installed 26 Feb. 1709, Chaplain in Ordinary to King William III &
Queen Mary II, Bishop of Chichester 13 Nov. 1709

CJ, x, 423; *ibid.*, 533; *ibid.*, 593; *ibid.*, 736; *Fasti Wynd.*, 49; *Al. Oxon. (1)*, iii, 966
DNB, xii, 960–1; *Hearne*, i, 396–7; *Luttrell*, vi, 380, 403, 409, 474, 478, 554; *Athenae*,
iv, 555; *Fasti Ox.*, ii, 334; *Nov. Rep.*, 90; *Rep. Eccl.*, i, 275; *Win. Schol.*, 191; *Bishop
Newton's Life (of Himself)*, ii, 177; *Cant. Acts*, iv, 461; *ibid*, v. 336

8 by 1694 VAUGHAN, Maurice
Appointed by Speaker Trevor. Address 21 April 1694
Son of Howell Vaughan
Born 1660 at Llanfyllin, Montgomery. *Died* 26 April 1722 (buried in
St George's Chapel Windsor)
Education: Eton, admitted pensioner at St John's Cambridge 1677
BA 1681 MA 1684
Fellow of Trinity Hall 1685–94
p. 1691
Rector of Yelling, Hants, 1692–1722, Prebendary of Lichfield
1692–1722, Canon of Windsor, installed 17 Feb. 1695

CJ, xi, 168; *Fasti Wynd.*, 69; *Al. Cant. (1)*, iv, 295; *Eton Reg. (2)*, 343

9 by 1695 BARTON, Samuel
Appointed by Speaker Foley. Addresses 29 April 1695, 20 April 1696
Son of the Revd John Barton of Harrietsham Kent
Born ? 1648 *Died* 15 August 1715 (buried in Westminster Abbey)
Education: Matric. as poor scholar Magdalen 1665, Scholar Corpus
Christi 1666.
BA 1669 MA 1673 BD 1682 DD 1697
Fellow of Corpus Christi Oxford 1682,
Rector of Great Brickhill Bucks 1680, Chaplain of St Saviour's
Southwark 1695, Prebendary of Westminster, installed 13 Feb. 1697,
Vicar of Christ Church with Rector of St Leonard Foster Lane,
London 1708

CJ, xi, 328; *ibid.*, 560; *Al. Oxon. (1)*, i, 81; *Hearne*, i, 221, 381; *Luttrell*, iv, 45, 178,
187–8; *Rep. Eccl.*, i, 922; *Nov. Rep.* 126, 448; *FEA*, iii, 363; *Athenae*, iv, 619; *Fasti Ox.*,
ii, 305, 380; *Cant. Acts*, vi, 195

10 by 1698 HALLIFAX, William
Appointed by Speaker Foley. Address 8 June 1698
Son of the Revd John Hallifax of Springthorpe, Lincolnshire
Born 1655 *Died* 1722

Education: Servitor at Brasenose Oxford 1670
Scholar and Fellow of Corpus Christi Oxford 1675
BA 1675   MA   1678   BD 1687   DD 1695
Chaplain to Levant Company at Aleppo 1685–95,
Rector of Old Swinford, Worcs. 1699–1722, Rector of Salwarpe,
Worcs. 1713–1722

CJ, xii, 302; *Al. Oxon. (1)*, ii, 636; *DNB*, viii, 999; *Hearne*, i, 221, 394; *Athenae*, iv, 620; *Fasti Ox.*, ii, 401; *BCR*, i, 224; *Cant. Acts*, vi, 116

11 **by 1699 GALLOWAY, William**
Appointed by Speaker Littleton. Address 15 April 1699
Son of John Galloway, a draper, of Oxford
Born ? 1660   *Died* 1716
Education: Matric. Hart Hall Cambridge 1674
BA 1678   MA 1681
Chaplain to the Officers of their Majesties (William III and Mary II)
Sea Train (i.e. Chaplain to the Marines), Vicar of Lindridge, Worcs.
1700–1716, Prebendary of Worcester 1710–16

CJ, xii, 644; *Hearne*, i, 221, 381; *FEA*, iii, 82; *Athenae*, iv, 794; *Parish Records Lindridge.*

12 **by 1701 HERN(E), John**
Appointed by Speaker Harley, Address 7 June 1701
Son of ? Hern of Tibenham Norfolk
Born ?   *Died* 24 April 1707
Education: Admitted pensioner at Clare Cambridge 1673
BA 1677   MA 1680   MA (Oxon) incorporated 1681   DD 1690
Fellow of Clare 1680
d. 1683
Rector of East Guildford, Sussex 1677–94, Rector of East Woodhay,
Hants 1691–1707, Chaplain to the King 1690, Canon of Windsor,
installed 16 Jan. 1690, Rector of East Shefford, Berks. 1694–1707

CJ, xiii, 601; *Al. Cant. (1)*, ii, 346; *Al. Oxon. (1)*, ii, 697; *Fasti Wynd.*, 95; *Luttrell*, vi, 169.

13 **by 1702 GASTRELL, Francis**
Appointed by Speaker Harley. Addresses 4 March 1702, 10 March 1702
23 May 1702
Son of Henry Gastrell of Slapton, Northants
Born 10 May 1662   *Died* 24 Nov. 1725 at Oxford (buried and memorial in Christ Church)
Education: Westminster, elected Student of Christ Church Oxford 1680
BA 1684   MA 1687   BD 1694   DD 1700
d. 1689   p. 1690
Preacher at Lincoln's Inn 1694–1714, Canon of Christ Church,
installed Jan. 1703, Proctor in Convocation 1711, Chaplain in Ordinary
to the Queen 1711, Bishop of Chester 14 April 1714

CJ, xiii, 775; *ibid.*, 786; *ibid.*, 907; *DNB*, xxi, 937–8; *Al. Oxon. (1)*, ii, 552; *Hearne*, i, 321; *Chetham Society Remains*, 21, 1850, iii–lxi; *Luttrell*, v. 240, 253, 382; *Athenae, Life*, lxxvii; *ROW*, i, 366; *Bio. Brit.*, iii, 2151–3

14 by 1704 STRATFORD, William

Appointed by Speaker Harley. Addresses 24 Feb. 1704, 23 Feb. 1705
Son of Nicholas Stratford, Bishop of Chester
Born ? 1672   *Died* 7 May 1729 (buried in Christ Church Oxford)
Education: Westminster (KS 1683), Matric. Christ Church Oxford 1688
BA 1692   MA 1695   BD 1703   DD 1705
Canon of Christ Church, installed 4 July 1703, Archdeacon of Richmond
10 Sept 1703, Rector of Little Shefford, Berks. 1707
Chaplain to Robert 1st Earl of Oxford and tutor to his son Edward Harley (i.e. Speaker Harley and his son) by 1711

CJ, xiv, 353; *ibid.*, 547; *Al. Oxon. (1)*, iv, 1435; *Hearne*, i, 5, 343; *Luttrell*, v. 394; *FEA*, ii, 531, iii, 267; *ROW*, ii, 891; *DNB*, viii, 1278–1280, 1283–90

15 by 1705 GODDARD, Thomas

Appointed by Speaker Smith. Addresses 18 Feb. 1706, 18 March 1707
Son of Edward Goddard of Tidworth, Wilts.
Born ? 1672   *Died* 10 May 1731 at Bath
Education: St Mary's Hall Oxford 1689, Magdalen Oxford
BA 1692   MA 1695
Rector of North Wraxall, Wilts. 1697–1708, Rector of North Tidworth, Wilts. 1708–31, Rector of St Benet Fink, London 1725, Canon of Windsor, installed 21 May 1707

CJ, xv, 158; *ibid.*, 345; *Al. Oxon. (1)*, ii, 576; *Hearne*, i, 82; *Luttrell*, v, 606; *ibid.*, vi, 169; *Fasti Wynd.*, 95; *Cant. Acts*, v, 278

16 by 1708 BRODRICK, Laurence

Appointed by Speaker Onslow. Address 10 March 1709
Son of Sir St John Brodrick of Wandsworth, Surrey
Born ?   *Died* 1747 at Kensington (buried at Mixbury 6 Nov. 1747)
Education: Kingston on Thames, admitted pensioner Trinity Cambridge 1687
BA 1691   MA 1694   DD 1710
d. 1693   p. 1694
Fellow of Kings 1695, Chaplain 1696
Vicar of Sandon, Herts. 1697–1711 Vicar of Meopham, Kent 1713–42
Prebendary of Westminster, installed 17 July 1710, resigned 1746,
Rector of Mixbury, Oxon 1713–43, Rector of Turweston, Bucks. 1714–41, Rector of Islip 1741–1747

CJ, xvi, 149; *WAR*, 79; *Al. Cant. (1)*, i, 223; *Luttrell*, vi, 375, 582, 601; *FEA*, iii, 364; *Nov. Rep.*, 448; *WAM*, 52223; *Cant. Acts*, vi, 135; *ibid.*, viii, 184

17 1710 KIMBERLEY, Jonathan

Appointed by Speaker Bromley. Address 15 May 1711
Son of William Kimberley of Bromsgrove, Worcs.
Born ? 1651   *Died* 7 March 1720
Education: Matric. Pembroke College Oxford 1667
BA 1671   MA 1674   MA (Cantab) incorporated 1676   DD 1713
Minister of Stadhampton, Oxon, Vicar of Trinity Church Coventry 1681–1713, Chaplain to Charles II (before 1685), Canon of Lichfield

1684–1713, Rector of Bagginton 1699, Vicar of Leamington Hastings
1712, Proctor in Convocation, Prebendary of Westminster 27 Sept.
1711, Dean of Lichfield 1713–20, Rector of Tatenhill, Staffs. 1713–20

CJ, xvi, 664; *Al. Oxon. (1)*, 850; *Al. Cant. (1)*, iii, 16; *Hearne*, ii, 104; *Luttrell*, vi, 659;
FEA, iii, 364 and i, 564; *Athenae*, iv, 749; *Fasti*, ii, 327, 335; *Nov. Rep.*, 448

18 by 1714 PELLING, John

Appointed by Speaker Hanmer. Address 14 June 1714, 18 Aug. 1714
Son of John Pelling of London
Born 17 Nov. 1670   *Died* 30 March 1750
Education: Matric. Christ Church Oxford 1686
BA 1690   MA 1693   BD 1702   DD 1703
Proctor 1701, Rector of St Anne Soho 1704–50, Prebendary of
Tottenhall or Tottenham Court in St Paul's 1705–50, Canon of
Windsor, installed 13 May 1715

CJ, xvii, 683; *ibid.*, xviii, 10; *Fasti Wynd.*, 113; *Hearne*, v, 60; *Al. Oxon. (1)*, iii, 1139;
Luttrell, vi, 394; *Athenae*, Life, ccxxii; *Nov. Rep.*, 51, 400; *GM*, xx, 139

19 by 1715 BARKER, Henry (or Harry)

Appointed by Speaker Compton. Address 5 July 1715
Son of Joseph Barker, Vicar of Sherborne, Dorset
Born ? 1657   *Died* 5 Sept. 1740 (buried in Westminster Abbey)
Education: Matric. Trinity Oxford 1673
BA 1676   MA 1679   BD 1689   DD 1713
?Rector of Stoke, Lincs. 1699–1720, Vicar of Pinchbeck, Lincs
1699–1720, Rector of Rotherfield Greys, Oxford, 1720–1740,
Prebendary of Westminster, installed 21 July 1716

CJ, xviii, 201; *WAR*, 357; *Al. Ox. (1)*, i, 70; *FEA*, iii, 364; *Nov. Rep.*, 448; *Cant. Acts*,
iv, 601; *GM*, x, 469, 525

20 by 1719 MANNINGHAM, Thomas

Appointed by Speaker Compton. Address 20 March 1719
Son of Thomas Manningham, Rector of East Tisted, Hants., later
Bishop of Chichester. Speaker's Chaplain 1690–4.
Born 1684 at East Tisted   *Died* 4 May 1750 (buried at Slinfold)
Education: Matric. King's Cambridge 1701
BA 1706   MA 1709   DD 1724
Fellow of King's 1704
d. 1708   p. 1709
Rector of St Peter's Slinfold and Selsey, Sussex 1711–1750, Chaplain to
the Bishop of Ely, Prebendary of Chichester 1711–1750, Canon
Treasurer 1712–1750, Prebendary of Westminster, installed 11 May 1720

CJ, xix, 135; *WAR*, 339, 381; *Al. Cant. (1)*, iii, 136; *FEA*, iii, 364; *GM*, xx, 236; *Nov.
Rep.*, 448; *Parish Records Slinfold.*

21 by 1723 INGRAM, George

Appointed by Speaker Compton. Address 23 May 1723
Son of Arthur 3rd Viscount Irvine
Born ? 1694   *Died* 14 April 1763 at Westminster

Education: Matric. Oriel College Oxford 1711
BA 1714   MA 1717
Fellow of Oriel 1716
Rector of Crudwell, Wilts. 1719–1763, Vicar of Hankerton, Wilts.
1723–1763, Prebendary of Westminster installed, 17 Oct. 1724
8th Viscount Irvine 1761

CJ, xx, 221; *Al. Oxon. (1)*, ii, 787; *FEA*, iii, 365; *Nov. Rep.*, 448; *Cant. Acts*, vii, 38; *GEC*, vii, 75; *GM*, xxiii, 201

22 by 1729 KENDRICK, Scawen

Appointed by Speaker Onslow. Address 22 Jan. 1729
Son of John Kendrick merchant of London.
Born 3 June 1694   *Died* 2 May 1753 (buried at Hambleden)
Education: Merchant Taylors' School, admitted Corpus Christi
Cambridge 1713
BA 1717   MA 1720   DD 1728
d. 1718   p. 1720
Vicar of Stone, Bucks. 1720, Rector of Hambleden 1722–53, Prebendary
of Westminster, installed 25 Nov. 1729, Archdeacon 1734, Sub-Dean
1743–53, Curate of St Margaret's Westminster 1730–53

CJ, xxi, 190; *Al. Cant. (1)*, iii, 8; *FEA*, iii, 365; *Hist. Reg.*, xiv, 15 Nov. 1729; *N&Q*, 6th series., viii, 10; *Nov. Rep.*, 439, 448; *GM*, xxiii, 248; Charles J. Robinson, *A Register of the Scholars admitted into Merchant Taylors' School AD 1562 to 1874*, 1883, ii, 20

23 1732 STEPHENS, George

Appointed by Speaker Onslow. Address 25 May 1732
Son of Henry Stephens of Overton Wiltshire
Born ? 1686   *Died* 18 Jan. 1751 (buried St George's Windsor)
Education: Salisbury, Matric. Trinity Cambridge 1770
BA 1703   MA 1710
d. 1706
Chaplain to Bishop of St Asaph, Rector of West Clandon, Surrey
1725–50, Vicar of All Saints' Isleworth 1746–51, Chaplain to Lord
Onslow (cousin of Speaker), Canon of Windsor, installed 17 May 1735

CJ, xxi, 934; *FW*, 62; *GM*, ii, 588; *ibid.*, v, 277; *ibid.*, xxi, 42; *Hist. Reg.*, xvii, 24 Jan. 1732; *Nov. Rep.*, 229; *Al. Cant. (1)*, iv, 155; *Trinity*, ii, 608; *Parish Records West Clandon.*

24 by 1736 BURCHETT, William

Appointed by Speaker Onslow. Address 18 May 1736
?Son of Josiah Burchett, body servant of Pepys who became secretary
to the Admiralty and MP for Sandwich
Born 1694   *Died* 27 Dec. 1750 (buried at Clewer)
Education: Eton, admitted pensioner Peterhouse Cambridge 1712
BA 1716   MA 1719
d. 1727
Assistant at Eton c. 1718–28, Vicar of Clewer 1729–50, Canon of
Windsor, installed 26 May 1739

CJ, xxii, 716; *Fasti Wynd.*, 70; *Al. Cant. (1)*, i, 255; *N&Q*, 4th series, xii, 388; *ibid.*, 5th series, vi, 468; *Eton Reg (1)*, i, 52; *GM*, ix, 273, *ibid.*, xxi, 42.

25 1739 TERRICK, Richard
Appointed by Speaker Onslow. Address 24 Jan. 1740
Son of Samuel Terrick, Rector of Wheldrake and Canon of York
Born (baptism York Minster 20 July 1710)   *Died* 31 March 1777
Education: Admitted pensioner Clare College Cambridge 1726
BA 1729   MA 1733   DD 1747
Fellow of Clare 1731–38
d. 1732   p. 1734
Preacher at Rolls Chapel London 1736–57, Chaplain in Ordinary to
the King 1745–57, Canon of Windsor, installed 16 June 1742, Vicar of
Twickenham 1742–1764,
Prebendary of Ealdland and Canon-Residentiary at St Paul's, installed
7 Oct. 1742, Master of the Temple 1748–53, Bishop of Peterborough 3
July 1757, Bishop of London 6 June 1764–1777.

CJ, xxiii, 428; *DNB*, xix, 558; *Lit. Anec.*, ix, 583–4; *Al. Cant. (1)*, iv, 215; *Nov. Rep.*, 3,
25, 57, 58, 431; *GM*, ix, 273

26 1742 YOUNG, Arthur
Appointed by Speaker Onslow. Address 15 April 1743
Son of Bartholomew Young of Bradfield Combust, Suffolk
Born 1693   *Died* 26 June 1759 at Bradfield Combust
Education: Admitted pensioner Pembroke Hall Cambridge 1711
LLB   1716   LLD 1728
d. 1716, p. 1717
Rector of Bradfield Combust and Rector of Bradfield St Clare 1719–59
Prebendary of Canterbury 27 June 1746, Vicar of Ixning, Suffolk
1748–59
J.P. for Suffolk

CJ, xxiv, 477; *DNB*, lxiii, 357; *Al. Cant. (1)*, iv, 492; *FEA*, i, 52; *GM*, xii, 331, xxix,
346; *CCR*, (1746), 70; *Cant. Acts*, viii, 389, 410; *ibid.*, ix, 365

27 1746 FULHAM, John
Appointed by Speaker Onslow. Address 7 May 1747
Son of John Fulham of Compton, Surrey
Born 1699   *Died* 13 July 1777 (buried at Compton)
Education: Eton College, Matric. Christ Church Oxford 1717
BA 1720   MA (Magdalene Cambridge) 1736
Rector of Compton 1722–77, Rector of Morrow 1736–52,
Prebendary of Chichester 1745–73, Archdeacon of Llandaff 1749–77,
Canon of Windsor, installed 17 April 1750, Vicar of All Saints'
Isleworth 1751–77

CJ, xxv, 376; *Fasti Wynd.*, 113; *Al. Cant. (1)*, ii, 183; *Al. Oxon. (2)*, ii, 500; *GM*, xvi,
384; *ibid.*, xxi, 42; *ibid.*, xlvii, 352; *CCR* (1750), 72; *Nov. Rep.*, 229; *Eton Reg. (1)*, i, 153;
Cant. Acts, xi, 164; C.A.H. Green, *Notes on the Churches in the Diocese of Llandaff*, 1906,
i, 7

28 1751 COPE, Richard
Appointed by Speaker Onslow. Address 13 June 1751
Son of Galen Cope, Rector of Eversley Hants (his mother Janet was
daughter of Richard Onslow kinsman of Speaker)

Born 1719   *Died* 6 Nov. 1806 at Cheltenham
Education: Admitted pensioner Clare Cambridge 1740
BA 1744   MA 1747   DD 1765
p. 1746
Rector of Eversley, Hants. 1745–1806, Prebendary of Westminster, installed 27 April 1754, Prebendary of Wells 1760, Rector of Islip 1767–1806,
Succeeded as 9th Baronet of Hanwell, Oxon and Bramshill, Hants. 1779

CJ, xxvi, 290; *Al. Cant. (1)*, i, 393; *FEA*, iii, 366; *CCR*, (1752), 72; *Nov. Rep.*, 449; *Burke Peer.* (1938), 648; *GM*, xxi, 42; *ibid.*, lxxvi (ii), 1176; Diana McClatchey, *Oxfordshire Clergy 1777–1869*, 1960, 49; *Cant. Acts*, x, 200.

29 1754 BALLARD, Reeve

Appointed by Speaker Onslow. Address 29 April 1755
Son of George Ballard of Surrey
Born ? 1713   *Died* 27 June 1770 at Bookham
Education: Matric. Christ Church Oxford 1730
BA 1734   MA 1738   DD (Lambeth) 1763
Vicar of Great Bookham (before 1754)–1769, Rector of Stoke D'Abernon, Surrey, 1754–69, Prebendary of Westminster, installed 8 July 1758, Vicar of St Bride's Fleet Street 1769–70

CJ, xxvii, 290; *Al. Oxon. (2)*, i, 55; *FEA*, iii, 366; *CCR*, (1755), 72; *Cant. Acts*, ix, 167; *ibid.*, x, 258; *Nov. Rep.*, 114, 449; *GM*, xl, 345

30 1758 BURDETT, Charles

Appointed by Speaker Onslow. Addresses 29 May 1759,
13 March 1761
Son of Charles Burdett of St Helen, London
Born ? 1700   *Died* 1 Dec. 1772
Education: Matric. Lincoln Oxford 1715
BA 1719   MA 1722   BD 1764   DD 1764
Rector of Holy Trinity and St Mary Guildford 1756–72, Rector of Worth, Sussex 1764–67, Prebendary of Westminster, installed 26 June 1762, Rector of Bokeham, Surrey 1767–72

CJ, xxviii, 599; *ibid.*, 1106; *FEA*, iii, 367; *CCR* (1759), 22; *Nov. Rep.*, 449; *Al. Oxon. (2)*, i, 191; *Guildford Parish Records; GM*, xxviii, 613; *ibid.*, xlii, 599

31 1761 CUST, Richard

Appointed by Speaker Cust (his brother). Address 20 May 1762
Son of Sir Richard Cust, Bart. of Leasingham, County Durham
Born ? 1728   *Died* 16 Oct. 1783
Education: Matric. Merton Oxford 1745
BA 1749   MA 1752   BD 1763   DD 1763
Rector of Belton, Lincs. (before 1770)–79, Rector of Fulbeck 1770–79, Canon of Christ Church Oxford Oct. 1765, Dean of Rochester 1779, Dean of Lincoln 22 Dec. 1782

CJ, xxix, 345; *Al. Oxon. (2)*, i, 331; *FEA*, ii, 36, 531, 579; *GM*, xxxi, 605; *ibid.*, xlix, 272; *CCR* (1762), 22; *Cant. Acts*, x, 318; *Cust*, iii, 77, 243; Francis Hill, *Georgian Lincoln*, 1966, 45–6

32 1765 PALMER, Richard
Appointed by Speaker Cust. Address 14 May 1766
Son of Henry Palmer of Lincolnshire
Born ? 1715   *Died* 7 May 1805 at Grantham
Education: Admitted Sizar Jesus Cambridge 1732
BA 1736   MA 1766   DD (Lambeth) 1770
d. 1737 p. 1740
Rector of Scott Willoughby, Lincs. 1740–1805, Rector of Adisham
1740–69, Rector of St Swithin London Stone, London 1776–1805,
Prebendary of Chichester 1769–81

CJ, xxx, 823; *Al. Cant. (1)*, iii, 301; *FEA*, i, 52; *CCR* (1769), 22; *Nov. Rep.*, 389; *Cant. Acts*, x, 309; *ibid.*, xi, 286, 288; *GM*, lxxv, 493; *Cust*, iii, 78, 262, 283

33 1770 BARFORD, William
Appointed by Speaker Cust (not continued by Norton). Address
9 May 1770
Son of the Revd Thomas Barford, Rector of Charlbury, Dorset
Born ? Baptised 2 Sept 1719 at Charlbury   *Died* November 1792 at
Kimpton
Education: Eton, Scholar King's Cambridge 1738
BA 1743   MA 1746   DD 1771
Fellow of King's 1741–63, Proctor 1761, Public Orator 1762–8
Tutor at King's 1746–70
d. 1742
PC of North Newton, Somerset 1722–31, Rector of Chilmark Wilts.
1723–47, Rector of Bishopston, Wilts. 1747–80, Vicar of Milton
Cambs. 1751, Vicar of Fordingbridge, Hants. 1768–73, Prebendary of
North Alton, Salisbury 1754, Canon of Canterbury June 1770, Rector
of Kimpton, Herts. 1773–92, Rector of All Hallows Lombard Street,
London 1778–92, Fellow of Eton College 1784–92

CJ, xxxii, 969; *DNB*, iii, 182–3; *Al. Cant. (1)*, i, 84; *FEA*, i, 55; *GM, lxii, 1155–1218; ibid., lxiii, 418–9; CCR* (1770), 68; *Nov. Rep.*, 79; *FES*, ii, 354; *Eton List*, ix a; *Eton Reg. (1)*, i; *Cant. Acts*, x, 307; *ibid.*, xi, 186, 187; *The Shorthand Diary of the Revd Joseph Price, 1770*, 31 (Public Library, Canterbury)

34 1770 KING James
Appointed by Speaker Norton. Addresses 30 April 1771,
15 May 1772 (his wife was Speaker Norton's sister)
Son of Thomas King of Skellands, Kirkby Malhamdale, Yorkshire
Born 1713   *Died* 24 April 1795 at Woodstock, Oxford
Education: Ripon, Matric. St John's Cambridge 1734
BA 1738   MA 1741   DD 1771
d. 1738, p. 1740
Vicar of Clitheroe and Downham, Lancs. 1743–50
Rector of Holy Trinity and St Mary Guildford 1772–4, Rector of
Dunsfold 1774–6
Canon of Windsor, installed 20 June, 1774 resigned 1776,
Dean of Raphoe 1776–95

CJ, xxxiii, 364; *ibid.*, 764; *Fasti Wynd.*, 79; *Al. Cant. (1)*, iii, 19; *RK*, (1771), 68; *Burke LG*, (1937), 1294; *FEH*, iii, 363; *GM*, xliv, 287; *ibid.*, lxv(i), 441; J. B. Leslie, *Raphoe Clergy and Parishes*, 1940, 17; *Price Diary, op. cit.*, 31

35 1774 ONSLOW, Arthur
Appointed by Speaker Norton. Addresses 17 May 1775,
14 May 1776
Son of Lt. Gen. Richard Onslow of St Anne Soho (and nephew of
Speaker Onslow)
Born 30 August 1746   *Died* 15 Oct. 1817 at Lindridge
Education: Eton, Matric. Exeter Oxford 1767
BA 1767   MA 1771   BD 1780   DD 1781
Fellow of All Souls
d. 1770, p. 1774
Rector of St James Garlickhithe 1776–87, Canon of Christ Church
1779–95, Rector of Maidenhead 1782–1817, Archdeacon of Berkshire
1785, Dean of Worcester 1795–1817, Vicar of Kidderminster
1795–1801, Vicar of Wolverley 1796–1811, Rector of Lindridge
1811–1817

CJ, xxxv, 381; *ibid.,* 796; *Al. Oxon. (2),* iii, 1042; *FEA,* ii, 531; *ibid.,* iii, 73; *Nov. Rep.,*
248; *GM,* xliv, 287; *ibid.,* lxxxvii, 474, 639; Bertram H. Green, *Bishops and Deans of
Worcester,* n.d. (?1957), 54; F. E. Hutchinson, *Worcester Monuments,* 1944, 144; John
Chambers, *Biographical Illustration of Worcestershire,* 1820, 533–536

36 1779 ALLANSON, Cuthbert
Appointed by Speaker Norton (no address, Allanson died in office)
Son of John Allanson of Preston, Lancs.
Born 21 Aug. 1725 at Chorley Lancs.   *Died* 3 June 1780 (buried at
Marston, Yorks.)
Education: Matric. Brasenose Oxford 1743
BA 1747   MA 1778   BD 1778   DD 1778
Rector of Upham, Hants. 1749–56, Rector of Wath, Yorks. 1756–80,
Prebendary of Ripon 1774–80

Al. Oxon. (2), i, 16; *GM,* (1780), l, 299; *CCR,* (1780), 66; *Fasti Rip.,* 310–1; *BCR,* 336

37 1780 WELFITT, William
Appointed by Speaker Norton. Address 31 May 1782
Son of William Welfitt of Hull
Born ? 1745   *Died* 3 Feb 1833 at Canterbury
Education: Matric. University College Oxford 1764
BA 1768   MA 1772   BD 1782   DD 1782
Rector of Blyborough with Bland, Leicestershire 1773–1786,
Rector of St Benet Gracechurch Street 1791 [? not in *Nov. Rep.*],
Rector of Hastingleigh, 1795, Vicar of Elmstead Kent, Vicar of
Tilehurst, Sussex 1795, Canon of Canterbury 7 Dec 1786

CJ, xxxviii, 1037; *FEA,* i, 50; *GM,* (1780), l, 447; *ibid.,* ciii (i), 282; Egerton Brydges,
Autobiography, i, 1834, 39–40; *Al. Ox. (2),* iv, 1521

**38 1780 CORNEWALL (from 1783 WALKER CORNEWALL)
Folliott Herbert**
Appointed by Speaker Cornwall (his second cousin). Addresses 3 July
1781, 10 July 1783
Son of Capt Frederick Cornewall RN of Delbury, Salop, MP for
Leominster

Born 1754   *Died* 5 Sept 1831 at Hartlebury (buried at Delbury)
Education: Eton, admitted pensioner St John's Cambridge 1772
BA 1777   MA 1780   DD (Lambeth) 1793
Fellow of St John's 1777–84
d. 1777, p. 1778
Rector of Frisham, Bucks. 1781–4, Canon of Windsor, installed 15
April 1784, Rector of East and West Rudham, Norfolk 1786–8, Master
of Wyggeston Hospital Leicester 1790–3,
Dean of Canterbury 1793–7,
Bishop of Bristol 1797–1803, Hereford 1803–8, Worcester 1808–31

CJ, xxxviii, 554; *ibid.*, xxxix, 697; *DECH*, 278; *Al. Cant. (2)*, ii, 138; *FEA*, i, 35, 221,
474; *ibid.*, iii, 69; *RK* (1781), 68; *Fasti Wynd.*, 89; *DNB*, xii, 227; *GM*, ci(ii), 290, 370;
Eton Reg. (1), ii, 126

39 1784 WILLIAMS, Philip

Appointed by Speaker Cornwall May 1784. Addresses 16 Aug. 1784, 5
July 1786
Son of the Revd Philip Williams, Rector of Starston, Norfolk
Born ? 1740   *Died* 21 Dec. 1830 at Compton
Education: Matric. New College 1760
BA 1764   MA 1767   MA (Cantab) incorporated 1770
Rector of Compton, Hants 1781–1830, Rector of Gosberton, Lincs.
1781–1830, Canon of Canterbury 4 May 1789, Prebendary of
Winchester 1797–1830

CJ, xl, 443; *ibid.*, xli, 965; *Al. Cant. (2)*, vi, 496; *Al. Oxon. (2)*, iv, 1568; *FEA*, i, 60,
iii, 41; *RK*, (1787) 69; *GM*, liv, 398; *ibid.*, ci, (ii), 186

40 1789 MOSS, Charles

Appointed by Speaker Grenville. Addresses 24 July 1789,
7 June 1790
Son of the Revd Charles Moss, Rector of St George Hanover Sq.
London (later Bishop of Bath and Wells)
Born 1763   *Died* 16 Dec. 1811 at Cuddesdon
Education: Matric. Christ Church Oxford 1780
BA 1783   MA 1766   BD 1797   DD 1797
Rector of Sherfield, Herts. 1786, Prebendary of Hurstbourn and
Burbage at Salisbury 1786, Prebendary of Wells 1786, Precentor of
Wells 1799, Prebendary of Westminster, installed 14 Aug. 1792
(resigned 1797), Canon Residentiary of St Paul's 1797–1807,
Prebendary of Consumpta-per-Mere 1797–1807, Bishop of Oxford
1807–11

CJ, xliv, 639; *ibid.*, xlv, 538; *DNB*, xiii, 1079; *Al. Oxon. (2)*, iii, 991; *FEA*, i, 158, 172,
198, 199, 207; *ibid.*, ii, 382, 509, 678; *ibid.*, iii, 368; *RK*, (1790), 69; *FES*, 396; *Nov.
Rep.*, 24, 58, 450; *GM*, lix, 379; *ibid.*, lxxxi (ii), 598, 668

41 1791 HAY, Thomas

Appointed by Speaker Addington. Addresses 3 June 1791, 16 June 1794
Son of Hon. Edward Hay of Lisbon, Son of 7th Earl of Kinnoull,
Minister Plenipotentiary at Lisbon
Born 14 May 1759   *Died* 29 Jan. 1830 at Christ Church Oxford
Education: Westminster (KS 1772), Matric. Christ Church Oxford 1776
BA 1780   MA 1783   BD 1795   DD 1795

Vicar of North Walsham, Norfolk ?–1790, Rector of Belton, Suffolk 1790–1830, Canon of Christ Church 1795–1830, Rector of North Repps 1813–1830

CJ., xlvi, 682; *ibid.*, xlix, 737; *Al. Oxon.* (2), ii, 632; *FEA*, ii, 531, *Burke Peer.*, 105 ed., (1980), i, 1511; *RK*, (1792), 69

42 1795 CAUSTON, Thomas

Appointed by Speaker Addington. Addresses 19 June 1795, 14 May 1796
Son of Charles Causton of Highgate
Born ?1758 *Died* 5 November 1842 at Bournemouth
Education Harrow, Pensioner St John's Cambridge 1787
BA 1791   MA 1794   DD 1820
d. 1791   p. 1792
Prebendary of Westminster, installed 26 March 1799
Rector of Turweston 1826–1842

CJ., l, 614; *ibid.*, li, 787; *Al. Cant.* (2), i, 541; *FEA*, iii, 368; *RK*, (1796), 69; *Nov. Rep.*, 450; *Harrow* (1). 51; *GM*, xix (n.s.), 103

43 1796 BUSBY, William Beaumont

Appointed by Speaker Addington. Addresses 17 July 1797, 11 July 1799, 29 Dec. 1800
Son of Tomlinson Busby of Hayes, Middlesex
Born 1757 at Hayes   *Died* 31 August 1820 at Killin, Scotland
Education: Matric. New College Oxford 1774
BA 1778   MA 1784   BD 1807   DD 1807
Prebendary of Canterbury 16 June 1802, Prebendary of Chichester 1802, Canon of Windsor, installed 23 July 1783, resigned 1808, Dean of Rochester 19 March 1808, Rector of West Farleigh 1816–20, Rector of Heyford Warren, Oxford 1816–20

CJ., lii, 743; *ibid.*, liv, 736; *ibid.*, lv, 927, *Fasti Wynd.*, 63; *Al. Oxon.* (2), i, 200, *FEA*, i, 56, 282; *ibid.*, ii, 579; *GM*, (1820), xc(2), 284; *RK*, (1797), 69, *Welsby*, 29

44 1801 BARTON, John

Appointed by Speaker Mitford, continued by Speaker Abbot 1802. Addresses 30 June 1801, 25 June 1802
Son of Newton Barton of Langley, Berks.
Born ? 1760   *Died* 17 Feb. 1803 at Sidmouth
Education: Matric. New College Oxford 1777
BA 1780   MA 1784
Rector of Sonning Berks., Rector of Chiddingford, Surrey, Prebendary of Canterbury Nov. 1802

CJ., lvi, 656; *ibid.*, lvii, 659; *Al. Oxon.* (2), i, 70; *FEA*, i, 60; *GM*, lxxiii (1), 285; *RK*, (1802), 89

45 1802 SMITH, Samuel

Appointed by Speaker Abbot. Addresses 6 Aug. 1803, 10 July 1805
Son of Revd Dr Samuel Smith, Headmaster of Westminster School
Born 20 Sept. 1765   *Died* 9 Jan. 1841 at Dry Drayton
Education: Westminster (KS 1777), Elected Christ Church Oxford 1782

BA 1786   MA 1789   BD 1797   DD 1808
Tutor and Censor 1794, PC of Daventry 1795, Prebendary of
Southwell 4 Nov. 1800, Prebendary of York 1801, Canon of Christ
Church 10 March 1807, Sub Dean 1809, Treasurer 1813, Dean of
Christ Church 1 March 1824, resigned 1831, Golden Stall at Durham 21
Sept. 1831, Rector of Dry Drayton, Cambs. 1831–41

CJ., lviii, 686; *ibid.*, lx, 486; *WAR*, 86; *Al. Oxon.* (2), iv, 1319; *RK*, (1804), 89; *FEA*,
iii, 192, 492, 319; *ibid.*, ii, 521, *ROW*, ii, 860; *GM*, xv (n.s.), 327

46 1806 BARNES, Frederick
Appointed by Speaker Abbot. Address 8 Aug. 1807
Son of the Revd Ralph Barnes, Canon of Exeter
Born ? 1771   *Died* 19 Aug. 1859 at Christ Church
Education: Westminster   (KS 1786), Christ Church Oxford 1790
BA 1794   MA 1797   BD 1805   DD 1811
Tutor and Censor 1802, Brigadier of Oxford Volunteer Corps 1803,
Junior Proctor 1804, Vicar of Colebrooke, Devon 1805, Vicar of
Colyton, Devon with PC of Monkton and Shute 1807–59, Rector of
Cheriton Bishop, Devon 1823–1844, Canon of Christ Church 17 Feb.
1810, Senior Canon from 1 April 1849, Sub Dean to Christmas 1852

CJ., lxii, 833; *MEB*, iv, 275; *Al. Oxon.* (2), i, 63; McClatchey, *op. cit.*, 173; *GM*, (1859),
vii (n.s.) (2), 426; *RK*, (1808), 104; *ROW*, i, 54 *FEA*, ii, 530; *Clergy List* (1847), 12;
Guardian, 24 Aug. 1859, 735

47 1807 PROBY, Charles
Appointed by Speaker Abbot. Addresses 10 Aug. 1807, 15 June 1809
Son of the Revd Dr Baptist Proby (later Dean of Lichfield)
Born 23 Jan. 1771 at Thornhaugh, Northants   *Died* 2 Feb. 1859 at
Twickenham
Education: Pensioner St John's Cambridge 1788
BA 1792   MA 1795
d. 1793   p. 1795
Curate of Tattenhall, Staffs. 1793–5, Curate of Thornhaugh with
Wansford 1795, Rector of Waddesdon, Bucks. 1800–23, Vicar of
Bishop's Tachbrook, Warwick 1803–59, Chaplain to Earl of Carysfort
1800–2, Chaplain to Duke of Marlborough 1803, Chaplain to Baroness
Seaforth 1818, Prebendary of Lafford (or Sleford), Lincoln 1808, Canon
of Windsor, installed 12 March 1814, Vicar of Twickenham 1818–59

CJ., lxii, 837; *ibid.*, lxiv, 407; *Fasti Wynd.*, 97; *Al. Cant. (2)*, v, 206; *Nov. Rep.*, 431;
Clergy List (1847), 193; *Guardian*, 9 Feb. 1859, 116; *Burke Peer.*, 105 ed., (1980), 2187;
GM, vii (n.s.) (2), 327

48 1812 WEBBER, James
Appointed by Speaker Abbot. Addresses 23 July 1812, 14 July 1813, 22
July 1814
Son of the Revd William Webber, Canon Residentiary of Chichester
Born ? 1772 at Winchester   *Died* 3 Sept. 1847 at Ripon (buried in
Cathedral)
Education: Westminster, Matric. Christ Church Oxford 1789
BA 1793   MA 1796   BD 1807   DD 1829

Tutor and Censor of Christ Church, Chaplain to Embassy at
Copenhagen 1795, Vicar of St Mary Magdalen Oxford 1803,
Prebendary of Strensal in York 1812–28, Vicar of Sutton-on-the-Forest,
Yorks. 1812–15, Rector of Kirkham, Lancs. 1813–47, Prebendary of
Ripon 1814, Prebendary of Westminster, installed 24 Feb. 1816, Curate
of St Margaret's 1828–35, Sub Dean 1828–35, Dean of Ripon, installed
24 Nov. 1828

CJ., lxvii, 548; *ibid.*, lxviii, 666; *ibid.*, lxix, 493; *WAR*, 93; *ROW*, ii, 976; *Al. Oxon.*
(2), iv, 1518; *RK (1813)*, 104; *IC (1815)*, 50; *FEA*, iii, 216, 332, 369; *Nov. Rep.*, 439,
450; *Clergy List (1847)*, 248; *Guardian*, 8 Sept. 1847, 563; *Fasti. Rip.*, 329; *GM*, xxviii,
(n.s.), 551

49 1815 STEVENS, Robert
Appointed by Speaker Abbot, continued by Speaker Manners Sutton
1817. Addresses 8 July 1817, 2 June 1818
Son of Robert Stevens of Norwich
Born 1777   *Died* 3 Feb. 1870 at Rochester Deanery (buried at West
Farleigh)
Education: Westminster, admitted pensioner Trinity Cambridge 1797
BA 1801   MA 1804   DD 1821
d. 1801   p. 1802
Lecturer at St Margaret's Westminster 1808–20, Rector of St James
Garlickhythe 1814–21, Vicar of West Farleigh 1820–70, Prebendary of
Lincoln 1814–70, Dean of Rochester 1820–70

CJ., lxxii, 466; *ibid.*, lxxiii, 410; *Al. Cant. (2)*, vi, 33; *MEB*, iii, 741; *RK (1817)*, 103;
FEA, ii, 159, 579; *ROW*, ii, 883; *Nov. Rep.*, 248; *Trinity*, iii, 367; *Welsby*, 29–30;
Guardian, 9 Feb. 1870, 151; Constance Hill, *Good Company in Old Westminster*
(Recollections of Anne (Rickman) Lefroy), 1925, 103; Ralph Arnold, *The Whiston*
Affair, 1961, *passim*

50 1818 WORDSWORTH, Christopher
Appointed by Speaker Manners Sutton. Address 12 July 1819
Son of John Wordsworth, Attorney-at-law of Cockermouth
Born 9 June 1774 at Cockermouth   *Died* 2 Feb. 1846 at Buxted
Education: Hawkshead G S, Cumberland, Matric. Trinity Cambridge
1792
BA 1796   MA 1799   DD 1810
Fellow of Trinity 1798
d. 1799   p. 1799
Rector of Ashby with Oby and Thurne, Norfolk 1804–5,
Domestic Chaplain to Archbishop of Canterbury 1805,
(Had been tutor to his son Charles at Trinity, who became Speaker
Manners Sutton)
Rector of Woodchurch, Kent 1806–8, Dean and Rector of Bocking
1808–15, Rector of St Mary Lambeth 1815–20, Rector of Sundridge,
Kent 1815–20, Master of Trinity 1820–41, Vice Chancellor of
Cambridge 1820–1, 1826–7, Rector of Buxted with Uckfield 1820–46

CJ., lxxiv, 633; *Al. Cant. (2)*, vi, 579; *DNB*, xx, 922; *RK (1820)*, 62; *FEA*, iii, 701, 612;
Guardian, 11 Feb 1846, 64; *Cantuar*, 257–8; *Trinity*, i, 14; *ibid*, iii, 328; *ibid*, iv, iv;
Wordsworth, 4–8

51 1819 BAYLAY, William Frederick
Appointed by Speaker Manners Sutton. Addresses 14 July 1820, 4 July
1821, 31 July 1822, 11 July 1823
Son of   ?Baylay of Devon
Born ? 1779   *Died* 5 January 1845 at Bishops Teignton, Devon
Education: Eton, admitted Fellow Commoner at Emmanuel 1797
BA 1802   MA 1805   MA (Oxon) incorporated 1834
Vicar of Dartmouth 1809–11, Vicar of St John Margate 1810–45,
Prebendary of Canterbury 1826–45, Prebendary of Rochester 1827,
Rural Dean 1840, Vicar of Wilmington, Kent 1828–32

CJ., lxxv, 454; *ibid.*, lxxvi, 501; *ibid.*, lxxvii, 477; *ibid.*, lxxviii, 475; *Al. Cant. (2)*, i,
193; *Al. Oxon. (2)*, i, 78; *FEA*, i, 49; *RK*, (1821), 89; *Eton List*, 14b, 21a; *GM*, xxiii,
(n.s.), 326

52 1824 MANNERS SUTTON, Thomas
Appointed by Speaker Manners Sutton (1st cousin of Thomas).
Addresses 19 June 1824, 30 June 1825, 19 May 1826
Son of John Manners Sutton of Kelham
Born 16 Aug. 1795   *Died* 27 Oct. 1844 at Averham, Notts.
Education: Eton, admitted pensioner Trinity Cambridge 1809
BA 1813   MA 1817
Prebendary of Westminster, installed 7 Dec. 1827, resigned 1831
Rector of Tunstall, Kent 1827–36, Rector of Great Chart 1818–36,
Prebendary of Lincoln 1831–44, Sub-Dean of Lincoln 1831–44
Rector of Averham with Kelham 1837–44

CJ., lxxix, 521; *ibid.*, lxxx, 622; *ibid.*, lxxxi, 374; *Al. Cant. (2)*, iv, 311; *GM*, (1844), xxii
(2), 663; *RK*, (1825), 89; *FEA*, iii, 369; *ibid.*, ii, 139, 42; *Nov. Rep.*, 450; *Eton List*, 49a;
Burke Peer., (1910) 350; *Trinity*, iv, 59

53 1827 SUTTON, Evelyn Levett
Appointed by Speaker Manners Sutton. Addresses 23 June 1827, 19 July
1828, 2 June 1829
Son of Evelyn Sutton of London
Born 10 June 1777   *Died* 26 Jan. 1835 (memorial in Westminster
Abbey)
Education: Hampstead School, admitted pensioner at Trinity Cambridge
1796
BA 1801   MA 1807
p. 1802
Rector of St Alphage Canterbury 1806–12, Vicar of High Halden, Kent
1812–15, Vicar of Preston, Kent 1812–17, PC of Oare 1817–25, Six
Preacher at Canterbury, Vicar of St Peter, Isle of Thanet, Prebendary
of Westminster, installed 7 Dec. 1827

CJ., lxxxii, 599; *ibid.*, lxxxiii, 547; *ibid.*, lxxxiv, 366; *Al. Cant. (2)*, vi, 86; *GM* (1835),
iii (n.s.), 554; *RK* (1826), 89; *FEA*, iii, 369; *Nov. Rep.*, 450; *Trinity*, iii, 362

54 1830 DAWSON, Francis
Appointed by Speaker Manners Sutton. Address 8 July 1830
Born ? 1788   *Died* 24 Oct. 1852 at Canterbury
Education: Admitted pensioner Trinity Cambridge 1807
BA 1812   MA 1816   BD 1825
d. 1812 p. 1813

Curate of Westwell, Kent 1812, Perpetual Curate of Folkestone
1813–15, Rector of Hawkinge 1813–15, Rector of Chislehurst 1815–46,
Rector of Orpington 1827, Rector of Hayes (Kent) 1827–31, Canon of
Canterbury 1833, Rector of All Hallows Lombard Street, London
1834–1846, Vicar of East Peckham 1846–52

CJ., lxxxv, 635; *Al. Cant. (2)*, ii, 255; *GM*, (1853), xxxix (n.s.), 214; *FEA*, i, 50; 79;
Clergy List (1847), 65; *Guardian*, 27 Oct. 1852, 711; *Trinity*, iv, 49

55 1830 LOCKWOOD, Frederick Vernon
Appointed by Manners Sutton. Address 13 Oct. 1831
Son of Thomas Lockwood of Dan-y-Craig, Glamorgan; mother,
daughter of Lord George Manners Sutton of Kelham
Born 1803 at Malden, Essex   *Died* (of smallpox caught visiting
parishioner) 1 July 1851 at Canterbury
Education: Eton, admitted pensioner Trinity Cambridge 1819
BA 1824   MA 1828
p. 1826
Curate of Sturry, Kent 1826–7, Rector of Mersham, Kent 1829–40,
Prebendary of Lincoln 1828–45, Canon of Canterbury 1838–51, Vicar
of Minster in Thanet, Kent 1839–51

CJ., lxxxvi, 909; *Al. Cant. (2)*, iv, 197; *MEB*, ii, 470; *FEA*, i, 53; *ibid.*, ii, 104, *RK*,
(1831), 89; *Clergy List* (1847), 151; *Guardian*, 9 July 1851, 499; *Eton List*, 93b; *Trinity*, iv,
165; *GM*, xxvi (n.s.), 215

56 1832 REPTON, Edward
Appointed by Speaker Manners Sutton. Address 10 Aug. 1832
Son of Humphrey Repton, garden designer of Sustead, Norfolk
Born 24 June 1782   *Died* 6 Aug. 1860 at St Leonards at Sea (buried at
Shoreham, memorial in vestry)
Education: Winchester, Matric. Wadham Oxford 1800, Magdalen 1801
BA 1804   MA 1806
Fellow of Magdalen
Rector of Miningsby, Lincs. 1817–1843, Perpetual Curate of St Philip,
Regent Street, London 1820–60, Prebendary of Westminster, installed
3 Nov. 1838, Vicar of Shoreham 1843–1860

CJ., lxxxvii, 578; *MEB*, iii, 116; *Al. Oxon. (2)*, iii, 1187; *IC* (1833), 57; *FEA*, iii, 370;
Nov. Rep., 252, 450; *WAR*, 97; *Win. Schol.*, 285; *Guardian*, 13 July 1859, 602; *ibid.*, 15
Aug. 1860, 734; *GM*, lx (n.s.), 321

57 1833 FRERE, Temple
Appointed by Manners Sutton. Address 23 Aug. 1833 (the last)
Son of John Frere of London & Roydon, MP for Norwich
Born 16 May 1781   *Died* 7 July 1859 at the Roydon Rectory
Education: Bury St Edmunds, Suffolk, admitted pensioner Trinity,
migrated to Downing, Cambridge 1797
BA 1802   MA 1805
Aberdeen University 1802–4
d. 1804   p. 1805
Curate of Woodbridge, Suffolk 1804–5, Curate of Roydon & Burston
1805–15, Rector of Finningham, Suffolk 1805–20, Curate of Little
Marlow, Bucks. 1815–21, Rector of Roydon & Burston 1820–59,

Prebendary of Westminster, installed 3 Nov. 1838, Resided at Roydon Hall 1821–46, JP for Norfolk 1823, for Suffolk 1829, DL for Norfolk 1826

CJ, lxxxviii, 716; *Al. Cant.* (2), ii, 580; *Burke LG*. 18 ed., (1969), 229; *RK*, (1834), 89; *FEA*, iii, 370; *Nov. Rep*, 450; *Guardian*, 13 July 1859, 602; *Trinity*, iii, 368; *GM*, vii (n.s.), 196

58 1835 VANE, John
Appointed by Speaker Abercromby
(Natural) Son of William Henry Vane, 1st Duke of Cleveland *(MEB)*
(Natural) Son of Robert Stewart, Viscount Castlereagh *(Dulwich College Register)*
Born 1792 *Died* 29 Dec. 1870 at Wrington, Somerset
Education: Westminster, admitted pensioner Trinity Cambridge 1809, migrated to Magdalene
BA 1814 MA 1817 BD ?
Fellow of Magdalene Cambridge 1814
Vicar of Wroxiter, Shropshire 1823–8, Rector of Wrington, Somerset 1828–70, PC of Burrington 1831–70, Preacher Rolls Chapel 1841–52, Chaplain in Ordinary to King William IV and then Queen Victoria 1831–70, Deputy Clerk of the Closet 1839–70, Fellow of Dulwich College 1818–48

Al. Cant. (2), vi, 276; *MEB*, vi, 734; *RK*, (1836), 90; *ROW*, ii, 943; *Records Chapel Royal*; *Guardian*, 4 Jan. 1871, 12; T. L. Ormiston, *Dulwich College Register 1619–1926*, 12; *Trinity*, iv, 60

59 1839 ANDREWES, Gerrard Thomas
Appointed by Speaker Shaw Lefevre
Son of the Revd Gerrard Andrewes (Dean of Canterbury 1809–25)
Born 27 Dec. 1794 *Died* 22 June 1851 in London, 8 Sackville St., Piccadilly (buried at Gt. Bookham)
Education: Westminster (KS 1809), admitted pensioner Trinity 1813
BA 1817 MA 1820
d. 1818 p. 1819
Rector of All Hallows Bread Street with St John the Evangelist London 1819–32, Six Preacher of Canterbury 1821–32, Clerk in Orders St James Westminster 1832–1851

Al. Cant. (2), i, 57; *MEB*, iv, 130–1; *GM*, (1839) xii (n.s.), 642; *RK*, (1840), 90; *ROW*, i, 19; *Nov. Rep.*, 76; *Guardian*, 25 June 1851, 459; *Trinity*, iv, 94, *GM*, xxxvi (n.s.), 215

60 1849 GARNIER, Thomas Parry
Appointed by Shaw Lefevre, March
Son of the Revd Thomas Garnier (Dean of Winchester 1840–1872)
Born 15 April 1809 at Bishop Stoke Rectory, Hants *Died* 7 Dec. 1863 at Lincoln Deanery
Education: Winchester, Worcester College, Oxford
BA 1830 BCL 1833
Fellow of All Souls 1830
d. 1833 p. 1834

Curate of Old Alresford, Hants 1834–35, Vicar of Lewknor 1835–40,
Rector of Longford, Derbyshire 1840–49, Chaplain of Lock Hospital
1849–50, Rector of Holy Trinity Marylebone 1850–59, Dean of Ripon
1859–60, Dean of Lincoln 26 April 1860

DNB, xxi, 9–10; *MEB*, i, 1125; *Al. Oxon.* (2), ii, 510; *RK*, (1854), 102; *Nov. Rep.*, 330;
Fasti Rip., 331–2; *Guardian*, 16 Dec 1863, 1166; *GM*, xvi (n.s.), 128, 240, 256; *ibid.*, xxxi
(n.s.), 310; *Wordsworth*, 58, 60, 71

61 1857 DRURY, Henry

Appointed by Speaker Denison
Son of the Revd Henry Joseph Thomas Drury, Master of the Lower
School at Harrow
Born 11 May 1812 at Harrow   *Died* 25 Jan. 1863 at Bremhill
Education: Harrow, Matric. Gonville and Caius Cambridge 1831
BA 1837   MA 1840
d. 1837   p. 1838
Classical Lecturer at Caius 1838–9,
PC of Alderley, Glos. 1839–40, Curate of Bremhill, Wilts 1840–3,
Rector of Alderley 1843–5, Vicar of Bremhill with Foxham and
Highway, Wilts. 1845–63,
Prebendary of Shipton, Salisbury 1855–63, Archdeacon of Wiltshire
1862–3

Al. Cant. (2), ii, 342; *DNB*, vi, 55–6; *MEB*, i, 921; *GM* (1857), iii (n.s.) 454; *ibid.*,
(1863), xiv (n.s.), 660; *RK*, (1858), 102; *FES*, i, 177; *ibid.*, ii, 418; *Guardian*, 28 Jan.
1863, 74; Percy M. Thornton, *Harrow School*, 1885, 282; *Harrow*, (2), 61

62 1863 MERIVALE, Charles

Appointed by Speaker Denison
Son of John Herman Merivale of Barton Place, Devon
Born 8 March 1808 in London   *Died* 27 Dec. 1893
Education: Harrow, Haileybury, admitted pensioner St John's
Cambridge 1826
BA 1830   MA 1833   BD 1840   DD 1871 Hon. LLD Edinburgh
1884 Hon. DCL Oxford 1866 Hon. DCL Durham
Fellow and Tutor St John's 1833–48 (Hon. Fellow 1874)
d. 1833   p. 1834
Preacher at Whitehall 1839–41, 1864, Select Preacher Cambridge
1838–40, Hulsean Lecturer 1862, Rector of Lawford, Essex 1848–70,
Dean of Ely 1869–93

Al. Cant. (2), iv, 394; *DNB*, xxii, 1035–6; *MEB*, ii, 849–50; *Clergy List* (1875), 248;
GM, (1850), ii, 423; *RK*, (1864), 102; *Denison*, 250; *Guardian*, 10 Jan. 1894, 61;
Harrow (2), 49; *Wordsworth*, 56

63 1869 WHITE, Henry

Appointed by Speaker Denison, continued by Speaker Brand 1872
Son of Edward White of Croydon, Surrey
Born 14 Feb. 1836   *Died* (in office, having resumed 1889) 7 Oct. 1890
Education: King's London, Censor 1867–9, Matric. Worcester
Oxford 1870, Fellow Commoner 1870
MA 1873, Fellow of King's London 1870

Curate of Dover 1858–9, Master of the Royal Chapel of the Savoy 1859–90, Hon. Chaplain to the Queen 1870–3, Chaplain-in-Ordinary to the Queen 1873–90, Lecturer in History Queen's London 1867–9

Al. Oxon. (2), iv, 1538; *MEB*, iii, 1311–12; *Clergy List,* (1875), 385; *RK*, (1870), 102; *Denison,* 251; *Vanity Fair,* 26 Dec. 1874

64 1874 BYNG, Francis Edmund Cecil
Appointed by Speaker Brand, continued by Speaker Peel 1884
Son of George Stevens, 2nd Earl of Strafford
Born 15 Jan. 1835   *Died* 18 Jan. 1918
Education: Eton, Matric. Christ Church Oxford 1852
BA 1857   MA 1858
d. 1858   p. 1859
Curate of Prestwich, Manchester 1858–9, Rector of Little Casterton, Rutland 1859–62, Vicar of Holy Trinity Twickenham 1862–67, Chaplain at Hampton Court 1867, Vicar of St Peter Cranley Gardens, South Kensington 1867–89, Hon. Chaplain to the Queen 1867–72, Chaplain-in-Ordinary to the Queen 1872–89, Resigned as Chaplain to the Speaker on succeeding as 5th Earl of Strafford 5 May 1889

Al. Oxon. (2), i, 206; *Clergy List* (1875), 568; *RK*, (1875), 96; *Eton List*, 218a, 228b; *Nov. Rep.*, 261, 432; *Crockford* (1916), 1468; *WWW*, (1916–28), 1006; *Burke Peer.*, 96 ed. (1938), 2339; *Vanity Fair*, 18 Oct. 1879

65 1889 WHITE, Henry
Appointed by Speaker Peel
previously Chaplain 1869–74
Died 7 October 1890 (in office) at 4 Lancaster Place, Strand
(for details see earlier entry no. 63)

66 1890 FARRAR, Frederic William
Appointed by Speaker Peel
Son of the Revd Charles Pinhorn Farrar, Chaplain of the Church Missionary Society
Born 7 Aug. 1831 in Bombay   *Died* 22 March 1903 at Canterbury (buried in Cathedral)
Education: King William's Isle of Man, King's London, Matric. Trinity Cambridge 1850
BA London 1852   BA Cantab 1854   MA 1857
BD 1872   DD 1874   FRS 1866
d. 1854   p. 1857
Fellow of Trinity 1856, Fellow of King's London,
Assistant Master Marlborough College 1853–55,
Harrow 1855–71, Hulsean Lecturer 1870,
Headmaster of Marlborough 1871–6,
Hon. Chaplain to the Queen 1869, Chaplain-in-Ordinary to the Queen 1873, Canon of Westminster, installed 9 May 1876, Rector of St Margaret's 1876–95, Archdeacon of Westminster 1883–95, Deputy Clerk of the Closet to Queen Victoria 1894–1901,
to King Edward VII 1901, Dean of Canterbury 1895–1903

DNB, 1901–11, ii, 9; *Nov. Rep.*, 439, 450; *ODCC* (ed. 2), 502; *RK*, (1891), 118; Reginald Farrar, *The Life of Frederic William Farrar*, 1904; Chadwick, ii, 27–8, 67;

A.M.G. Stephenson, *The Rise and Decline of English Modernism*, 1984 17, 43; *Guardian*, 10 Jan. 1894; *ibid.*, 25 March 1903, 435; *ibid.*, 1 April 1903, 471; K.S.S. Harrison, *King William's College Register*, 1928, 24, 459; *WWW*, (1897–1916), 238; *Trinity*, iv, 74, 649; Margaret Drabble, ed., *The Oxford Companion to English Literature*, 5 ed., 1985, 193, 324, 340; *Marlborough*, ix, xiii, xxi; *Vanity Fair*, 10 Oct. 1891

67 1896 WILBERFORCE, Albert Basil Orme
Appointed by Speaker Gully
Son of the Revd Samuel Wilberforce (later Dean of Westminster, Bishop of Oxford, Winchester)
Born 14 Feb. 1841 at Winchester   *Died* 13 May 1916 at Westminster
Education: Eton, Matric. Exeter Oxford 1860
BA 1865   MA 1867   BD 1894   DD 1894
d. 1867   p. 1868
Curate of Cuddesdon, Oxford 1866–7, Domestic Chaplain to Bishop of Oxford (his father) 1866–70, Curate of Seaton, Devon, Curate of St Jude Southsea 1869–71, Chaplain to Bishop of Winchester 1870–73, Rector of St Mary Southampton 1871–94, Hon. Canon Winchester 1876–94, Select preacher Oxford 1897–9, Canon of Westminster, installed 7 July 1894, Rector of St John's Smith Square Westminster 1894–1916, Archdeacon of Westminster 1900–1916

Al. Oxon. (2), iv, 1551; *IC*, (1897), 71; *Eton List*, 266b; *Nov. Rep.*, 451; *WWW*, (1916–28), 1124–5; David Newsome, *The Parting of Friends*, 1966, 24–5, 258; W.E. Russell, *Basil Wilberforce*, 1917; *Vanity Fair*, 6 Jan. 1909

68 1916 CARNEGIE, William Hartley
Appointed by Speaker Lowther, continued by Speaker Whitley 1921 and Fitzroy 1928
Son of Robert Carnegie of Teremore, Co Dublin
Born 1859   *Died* 18 Oct. 1936
Education: Matric. Demy Magdalen Oxford 1878
BA 1884   MA 1897
1885–7 travelling round the world yachting and shooting
d. 1887   p. 1888
Curate of St Paul's Pudsey 1887–8, Rector of Great Whitley 1889–1903, Rector of St Philip Birmingham 1903–12, Select Preacher Oxford 1905, Canon of Westminster, installed 1 April 1913, Rector of St Margaret's 1913–36, Archdeacon of Westminster 1918–9, Sub Dean 1919–36

Al. Oxon. (2), i, 220; *IC*, (1917), 222; *WWW*, (1929–40), 222; *Crockford* (1936), 208; J.L. Garvin, *The Life of Joseph Chamberlain*, 2, viii, ix, 338–9; F. R. Barry, *Period of My Life*, 1970, 114; *Don* (1936), 17, 22; *Times*, 23 May 1916, 9; *ibid.*, 21 Feb. 1936, 14

69 1936 DON, Alan Campbell
Appointed by Speaker Fitzroy, continued by Speaker Clifton Brown 1943
Son of Robert Bogle Don
Born 3 Jan. 1885 at Broughton Ferry   *Died* 3 May 1966
Education: Rugby, Magdalen Oxford, Cuddesdon Oxford
BA 1907   MA 1911   Hon DD St Andrews 1932
d. 1912   p. 1913
Curate St Peter Redcar 1912–16, Vicar of Norton-juxta-Malton, Yorks.

1917–21, Provost of St Paul's Cathedral Dundee 1921–31,
Chaplain and Secretary to Archbishop of Canterbury 1931–41,
Chaplain to the King 1934–46, to the Queen 1959–66,
Canon of Westminster, installed 25 Jan. 1941, Rector of St Margaret's
1941–46, Sub Dean 1941–46, Dean of Westminster 1946–59, Select
Preacher Oxford 1940–41, Cambridge 1942,
KCVO 1948

Times, 21 Feb. 1936, 14; *ibid.*, 30 July 1946, 7; *WWW*, (1961–70), 310; *IC*, (1936), 211;
CEYB, (1958), 201; J.G. Lockhart, *Cosmo Gordon Lang*, 1949, *passim*; *Don* (1936), 21ff.

70 1946 CHESHIRE, Christopher

Appointed by Speaker Clifton Brown, continued by Speaker Morrison
1951
Son of Walter Chevalier Cheshire
Born 3 Nov. 1881   *Died* 18 Oct. 1958
Education: St Catherine's Broxbourne, St John's College Oxford
BA 1904   MA 1909
d. 1904   p. 1905
Curate of St Anne Limehouse 1904–10, Curate of Hartfield with
Coleman's Hatch 1910–11, The Lickey with Barnet Green 1911–14,
Warden of Liddon House and Curate in Charge Grosvenor House
1914–24, Rector of Holy Trinity Sloane Square Chelsea 1924–45, Hon.
Chaplain to Archbishop of York 1928–42, Rural Dean of Chelsea
1932–45, Prebendary of Broomsbury in St Paul's 1941–58, Resident
Chaplain at Lambeth to Archbishop of Canterbury 1945–46

Times, 30 July 1946, 7; *ibid.*, 30 Nov. 1955, 12; *ibid.*, 21 Oct. 1958, 14; *IC*, (1947), 328;
Crockford, (1957–58), 203; Ann Callender, ed., *Godly Mayfair*, 1980, 21–6, 42

71 1955 CAMPBELL, John McLeod

Appointed by Speaker Morrison, continued by Speaker
Hylton Foster 1959
Son of the Revd D. Campbell of Oakford Rectory, Bampton, Devon
Born 6 July 1884   *Died* 26 Feb. 1961
Education: Marlborough, Balliol Oxford, Bishop's College Farnham
BA 1906   MA 1910   DD Lambeth 1946   Hon DD Glasgow 1954
d. 1909   p. 1910
Fellow and Chaplain Hartford College 1909–24
Temporary Chaplain to the Forces 1914–19, Senior Chaplain
4th Division BEF.   MC,
Principal Trinity College Kandy, Ceylon 1924–35, General Secretary
Overseas Council of the Church Assembly 1935–53, Hon. Canon
Canterbury 1936–61, Chaplain to the King 1944–52, to the Queen
1952–61, Master of Charterhouse 1954–61,

WWW, (1961–70), 175; *IC*, (1958), 321; *CEYB*, (1948), 198; *Crockford*, (1959–60), 176;
Marlborough, 557; *Don*, (1936), 29; Roger Lloyd, *The Church of England 1900–1965*,
1966, 580

72 1961 STANCLIFFE, Michael Staffurth

Appointed by Speaker Hylton Foster, continued by Speaker King 1965
Son of the Revd H.E. Stancliffe, Vicar of St John's Grantham (later
Canon and Prebendary of Lincoln)

Born 8 April 1916   *Died* 26 March 1987
Education: Haileybury, Trinity Oxford, Lincoln Theological College
BA 1938   Dip.Th. 1939   MA 1943
d. 1940   p. 1941
Curate of St James Southbroom Devizes 1940–43, Priest-in-Charge Ramsbury 1943–44, Curate of Cirencester and Priest-in-charge Holy Trinity Watermoor 1944–9, Chaplain and Master Westminster School 1949–57, Preacher Lincoln's Inn 1954–57, Canon of Westminster, installed 25 Jan. 1957, Rector of St Margaret's 1957–69, Dean of Winchester 1969–86

WW, (1987), 1657; *IC,* (1962), 85; *CEYB,* (1986), 371; *Crockford,* (1985–86), 459

73 1969 NEVILL, Thomas Seymour
Appointed by Speaker King, continued by Speaker Lloyd 1971
Son of T.G. Nevill
Born 30 Oct. 1901   *Died* 17 Aug. 1980
Education: Dover College, Jesus Cambridge, Westcott House Cambridge
BA 1923   MA 1926
Assistant Master, Llandovery College, Dover College, Weymouth College,
School Secretary of Student Christian Movement 1934–7,
Headmaster of Wellingborough School 1940–56,
d. 1956   p. 1957
Curate of Fareham Parish Church 1956–8, Charterhouse Mission in Southwark 1958–72, Master of Charterhouse 1962–73, Chaplain Royal Masonic Hospital 1973–78

WWW, (1971–80), 578; *IC,* (1971), 495; *Crockford,* (1977–9), 730

74 1972 EDWARDS, David Lawrence
Appointed by Speaker Lloyd, continued by Speaker Thomas 1976
Son of Lawrence Wright Edwards
Born 20 January 1929
Education: King's School Canterbury, Magdalen Oxford, Westcott House Cambridge
BA 1952   MA 1956   DD Lambeth 1989
Fellow of All Souls 1952–59
d. 1954   p. 1955
Tutor Westcott House 1954–55, Curate of St John Hampstead 1955–58, Student Christian Movement Secretary 1955–58, Curate of St Martin-in-the-Fields 1958–66, Editor SCM Press 1959–66, General Secretary SCM 1965–6, Dean of King's College Cambridge 1966–70, Six Preacher Canterbury 1969–76, Canon of Westminster, installed 20 July 1970, Rector of St Margaret's 1970–78, Sub Dean 1974–78, Dean of Norwich 1978–83,
Provost of Southwark 1983–

CEYB, (1990), 346–7; *Crockford,* (1989–90), 187; *WW,* (1990), 543; *IC,* (1973), 519

75 1978 BAKER, John Austin
Appointed by Speaker Thomas
Son of George Austin Baker
Born 11 Jan. 1928
Education: Marlborough, Oriel Oxford, Cuddesdon Oxford
BA 1952   MA 1955   M Litt 1955   DD Lambeth 1990
d. 1954   p. 1955
Curate of Cuddesdon and Tutor at Theological College 1954–7,
Curate of Hatch End and Asst Lecturer in Theology King's College
London, 1957–59, Fellow, Chaplain and Lecturer Corpus Christi
College Oxford 1959–73 (also Brasenose and Lincoln 1959–73 and
Exeter 1968–73), Canon of Westminster, installed 29 Sept. 1973,
Sub Dean 1978–82, Rector of St Margaret's 1978–82,
Bishop of Salisbury 1982–

CEYB, 1900, 381; *Crockford*, (1989–90), 26; *WW*, (1990), 1599; *CSYB*, (1979), 25

76 1982 BEESON, Trevor Randall
Appointed by Speaker Thomas, continued by Speaker Weatherill 1983
Son of Arthur William Beeson
Born 2 March 1926
Education: King's London, St Boniface Warminster
AKC 1950   MA Lambeth 1976
Fellow of King's London 1987
d. 1951   p. 1952
Curate of Leadgate Durham 1951–54, Priest-in-charge, then Vicar of St
Chad Stockton-on-Tees, Curate of St Martin-in-the-Fields 1965–71,
Editor *New Christian* 1965–70, Vicar of Ware 1971–76, Canon of
Westminster, installed 1 May 1976, Rector of St Margaret's 1982–87,
Dean of Winchester 1987–

CEYB, (1990), 331; *Crockford*, (1989–90), 44; *WW*, (1990), 125; *CSYB*, (1982), 23

77 1987 GRAY, Donald Clifford
Appointed by Speaker Weatherill
Son of Henry Hackett Gray
Born 21 July 1930
Education: Newton Heath Technical High School, King's London,
St Boniface Warminster
AKC, 1955   MPhil Liverpool 1980
PhD Manchester 1985   FRHistS 1988
d. 1956   p. 1957
TA & TAVR Chaplain 1958–77   TD 1970
Curate of Leigh Parish Church 1956–60, Vicar of St Peter Westleigh
1960–67, Vicar of All Saints' Elton 1967–74, Rector of Liverpool
1974–87, Rural Dean of Liverpool 1975–81, Canon Diocesan of
Liverpool 1982–87, Hon. Chaplain to the Queen 1974–77,
Chaplain to the Queen 1980–
Canon of Westminster, installed 14 March 1987
Rector St Margaret's 1987–

CEYB, (1987), 338; *Crockford,* (1989–90), 246; *WW*, (1990), 721; *CSYB*, (1990), 26

Form of prayers used in the House

This version is from the reign of George V

PRAYERS FOR THE PARLIAMENT.

PSALM LXVII.

GOD be merciful unto us, and bless us: and shew us the light of his countenance, and be merciful unto us.

That thy way may be known upon earth: thy saving health among all nations.

Let the people praise thee, O God: yea, let all the people praise thee.

O let the nations rejoice and be glad: for thou shalt judge the folk righteously, and govern the nations upon earth.

Let the people praise thee, O God: yea, let all the people praise thee.

Then shall the earth bring forth her increase: and God, even our own God, shall give us his blessing.

God shall bless us: and all the ends of the world shall fear him.

¶ *After the Psalm, these Suffrages, and the Prayers following, shall be used.*

THE Lord be with you.
  Answer. And with thy Spirit.

¶ Let us pray.

Lord, have mercy upon us.
  Christ, have mercy upon us.
Lord, have mercy upon us.

OUR Father, which art in Heaven, Hallowed be thy Name. Thy Kingdom come. Thy Will be done in Earth, as it is in Heaven. Give us this day our daily bread. And forgive us our trespasses, as we forgive them that trespass against us. And lead us not into temptation; But deliver us from evil. For thine is the Kingdom, the Power, and the Glory, for ever and ever. *Amen.*

O LORD our heavenly Father, high and mighty, King of kings, Lord of lords, the only Ruler of princes, who dost from thy throne behold all the dwellers upon earth; Most heartily we beseech thee with thy favour to behold our most gracious Sovereign Lord King GEORGE, and so replenish him with the grace of thy Holy Spirit, that he may alway incline to thy will, and

walk

Prayers for the Parliament.

walk in thy way: Endue him plenteously with heavenly gifts, grant him in health and wealth long to live, strengthen him that he may vanquish and overcome all his enemies; and finally after this life he may attain everlasting joy and felicity, through Jesus Christ our Lord. *Amen.*

ALMIGHTY God, the Fountain of all Goodness, we humbly beseech thee to bless our gracious Queen MARY, ALEXANDRA the Queen Mother, EDWARD Prince of Wales, and all the Royal Family: Endue them with thy Holy Spirit; enrich them with thy Heavenly Grace; prosper them with all happiness; and bring them to thine everlasting Kingdom, through Jesus Christ our Lord. *Amen.*

ALMIGHTY God, by whom alone Kings reign, and Princes decree justice; and from whom alone cometh all counsel, wisdom, and understanding; We thine unworthy servants, here gathered together in thy Name, do most humbly beseech thee to send down thy Heavenly Wisdom from above, to direct and guide us in all our consultations: And grant that, we having thy fear always before our eyes, and laying aside all private interests, prejudices, and partial affections, the result of all our counsels may be to the glory of thy blessed Name, the maintenance of true Religion and Justice, the safety, honour, and happiness of the King, the publick wealth, peace, and tranquillity of the Realm, and the uniting and knitting together of the hearts of all persons and estates within the same, in true Christian Love and Charity one towards another, through Jesus Christ our Lord and Saviour. *Amen.*

PREVENT us, O Lord, in all our doings, with thy most gracious favour, and further us with thy continual help, that in all our works begun, continued, and ended in thee, we may glorify thy Holy Name, and finally by thy mercy obtain everlasting Life, through Jesus Christ our Lord. *Amen.*

2 *Cor.* xiii. 14.

THE Grace of our Lord Jesus Christ, and the love of God, and the fellowship of the Holy Ghost, be with us all evermore. *Amen.*

LONDON:
Printed by VACHER & SONS, LTD., Westminster House, S.W.1.—11718.

Appendix II

The Speaker's Chaplain and *Vanity Fair*

T HE SPEAKER'S CHAPLAIN PROVED TO BE A POPULAR subject for the *Vanity Fair* caricaturists. First published on 7 November 1868, *Vanity Fair* included its first full-page coloured caricature (of Benjamin Disraeli) in its issue of 30 January 1869. Technically known as "chromolithographs" they boosted the sales of the periodical. As the caricature portraits grew in popularity it became the custom to publish annual albums of collected prints from the previous year. Subsequently the prints have become collector items.

They are often referred to as 'Spy cartoons', but they are not all by Sir Leslie Ward whose sobriquet was 'Spy'. The earliest cartoons were by Carlo Pellegrini who was 'Ape'. Each caricature was accompanied by a brief letterpress biographical sketch signed 'Jehu Junior'. During his editorship of *Vanity Fair* (1868–1889) these pen portraits were the work of Thomas Gibson Bowles.[1]

Henry White was the first Chaplain whose caricature appeared in *Vanity Fair*. It was in the issue of 26 December 1874, and it is by Pellegrini (i.e. 'Ape').[2] Although his sketches were done almost entirely from memory, Pellegrini would sometimes go to great lengths to get impressions.

> 'His Christmas offering of the Rev. Henry White,
> for example, required his taking the sacrament
> at the Savoy Chapel in order to get a 'close-up'
> of his 'victim'.[3]

Five years later the Honourable and Reverend Francis Byng was the subject of a 'Spy' cartoon.[4] Leslie Ward recalled in his autobiography, *Forty Years of 'Spy'*, that Byng was,

> 'a little man with great dignity,
> glossy curly black hair and a very prominent
> chin. He was a perfect study for the
> caricaturist, and I believe any thing but a
> stereotyped parson'.[5]

Archdeacon Farrar's portrait, also by 'Spy', appeared on 10 October 1891. 'Jehu Junior' described him on that occasion as 'a picture of comfortable piety'.[6]

The fourth and last Chaplain to be caricatured, and again by 'Spy', was

Archdeacon Basil Wilberforce.[7] Once again a Speaker's Chaplain made an impression on the artist Leslie Ward. He wrote:

'I had observed him in the House of Commons,
and in his beautiful and most interesting
home in Dean's Yard. His unrivalled stateliness
of bearing was combined with unusual lightness
of movement, and he was a most impressive
figure, especially on occasions of state
ceremonial. I remember watching him with
great pleasure in his place in the Speaker's
procession as it passed to the House for prayers.
There was no man in London who had such a
following in the pulpit. As a subject he was
most interesting and very patient. His gown
in the reproduction is the best sample of
three-colour work I had ever done, and he was so
pleased with my drawing that he bought it'.[8]

Select Bibliography

(place of publication is London unless otherwise stated)

Baldwin, David, The Chapel Royal: ancient and modern, 1990.

Bickersteth, John and, Dunning, Robert, *Clerks of the Closet in the Royal Household*, Stroud, 1991.

Boulton, Clifford J. (ed.) *Erskine May's Treatise on the Law, Privileges, Procedures and Usage of Parliament*, 21st ed., 1989.

Brigden, Susan *London and the Reformation*, Oxford, 1989.

Brightman, F.E. *The English Rite, being a synopsis of the sources and the revision of the Book of Common Prayer*, 1915.

Cannon, John *Parliamentary Reform, 1640–1832*, Cambridge, 1973.

Carpenter, Edward (ed.) *A House of Kings, The History of Westminster Abbey*, Revised ed. 1972.

Coates, Willson Havelock (ed.) *The Journal of Sir Simonds D'Ewes From the First Recess of the Long Parliament to the Withdrawal of King Charles from London*, New Haven, 1942.

Colvin, H.M. *The History of the King's Works*, vol. i, 1963.

Cuming, G.J. *A History of Anglican Liturgy*, 2nd ed., 1982.

Dasent, Arthur Irwin *The Speakers of the House of Commons from the Earliest Times to the Present Day with a Topographical Description of Westminster at Various Epochs and a Brief Record of the Principal Constitutional Changes during Seven Centuries*, 1911.

Dugdale, William *Monasticon Anglicanuum*, 1655–73 (new ed. 1846).

Edwards, David L. *St Margaret's Westminster*, 1973.

Graham, Harry *The Mother of Parliaments*, 1910.

Hastings, Maurice *Parliament House. The Chambers of the House of Commons*, 1950. *St Stephen's Chapel and its place in the development of Perpendicular Style in England*, 1955.

Laundy, Philip *The Office of Speaker*, 1964.

Liu, Tai *Puritan London, A Study of Religion and Society in the City Parishes*, Delaware, Newark, 1986.

McKay, W.R. *Secretaries to Mr. Speaker*, House of Commons Library Document No. 14, 1986.
Clerks in the House of Commons 1363–1989: A Biographical List, House of Lords Record Office Occasional Publications no. 3, 1989.
Observations, Rules and Orders of the House of Commons. An early procedural collection, House of Commons Library Document no. 17, 1989.

Marsden, Philip *The Officers of the Commons 1363–1978*, 1979.

Menhennet, David *The Journal of the House of Commons: A Bibliographical and Historical Guide*, House of Commons Library Document no. 7, 1971.

Parry, Charles H. *The Parliaments and Councils of England Chronologically arranged from the reign of William I to the Revolution in 1688*, 1839.

Porritt, Edward *The Unreformed House of Commons. Parliamentary Representation before 1832*, Cambridge, 1903.

Pronay, Nicholas and Taylor, John *Parliamentary Texts of the Later Middle Ages*, 1980.

Redlich, Josef (trans. A. Ernest Steinhal) *The Procedure of the House of Commons. A Study of its History and its Present Form*, 1908.

Roskell, J.S. *The Commons and their Speakers in English Parliaments 1376–1523*, Manchester, 1965.

Rosser, Gervase *Medieval Westminster 1200–1540*, Oxford, 1989.

Skottowe, B.C. *A Short History of Parliament*, 1892.

Smyth, Charles *Church and Parish, Studies in Church Problems illustrated from the Parochial History of St Margaret's Westminster*, The Bishop Paddock Lectures for 1953–4, 1955.

Thomas, P.D.G. *The House of Commons in the Eighteenth Century*, Oxford, 1971.

Thorne, Peter *Ceremonial and the Mace in the House of Commons*, House of Commons Library Document no. 11, 1980.

Westlake, H.F. *St Margaret's Westminster. The Church of the House of Commons*, 1914.

See also list of abbreviations (p. x) for works of reference frequently consulted

Notes

PART ONE

1 Chapels and Chaplains at Westminster

1 Frank Barlow, *Edward the Confessor*, 1970, p. 260.

2 Whether Edward was technically building afresh or actually 'rebuilding' on the site of an earlier Benedictine monastery on Thorney Island is a continuing historical debate. A good claim for an Abbey founded by St Dunstan c 960 can be made (C. A. Ralegh Radford, *Westminster Abbey before King Edward the Confessor*. Westminster Abbey Occasional Paper, XV, Summer 1965, p. 5), but, even so, there could have been an earlier Saxon Minster Church on the site ('the foundation of a minster here at some time after 700 would not be extraordinary'. Gervase Rosser, *Medieval Westminster 1200–1540*, 1989, p. 12). It can be confidently asserted that no monastery, as such, existed in Westminster before Dunstan's time. (Barbara Harvey, *Westminster Abbey and its Estates in the Middle Ages*, 1977, pp. 21–2).

3 Maurice Hastings, *Parliament House, The Chamber of the House of Commons*, 1950, p. 39.

4 J. M. Hastings, *St Stephen's Chapel and its place in the development of Perpendicular style in England*, 1955, p. 43.

5 David Hugh Farmer, *The Oxford Dictionary of Saints*, pp. 265–6.

6 Ed. C. T. Onions (with G. W. S. Friedrichson and R. W. Burchfield), *Oxford Dictionary of English Entymology*, 1966, p. 163.

7 E.g. Laon, Meaux, see Hastings, *St Stephen's, op. cit.*, p. 64.

8 *Ibid*, pp. 1–2; H. M. Colvin, *The History of the Kings Works*, 1963, vol. i, p. 510.

9 Hastings, *Parliament House, op. cit.*, p. 56; Paul Binski, *The Painted Chamber at Westminster*, The Society of Antiquaries of London, Occasional Paper (New Series) ix, 1986, p. 21 ff.

10 *VCH, London*, i, p. 566.

11 *Ecclesia Collegiata, sibe Capella Regis S. Stephani, infra Pallacium regale Westmonasterii* in William Dugdale, *Monasticon Anglicanuum*, 1655–73 (new ed. 1846), vol. viii, p. 1348.

12 *The Chapel of St Mary Undercroft in the Palace of Westminster*, House of Lords, HMSO 1978, *passim* (pages not numbered); Robert Cooke, *The Palace of Westminster: Houses of Parliament*, 1987, p. 222–3; Megan Aldrich in ed. Megan Aldrich, *The Craces: Royal Decorators 1768–1899*, Brighton, 1990, pp. 110–112.

13 An Acte whereby certaine Chauntries Colleges Free Chappelle and the Possessions of the same be given to the Kings majesty I Edw VI cap 14, *The Statutes of the Realm*, Vol. 4, pp. 24–33.

15 During the time of the 1834 fire, James Webber (Chaplain 1812) was visiting Westminster and sent his servant James to help fight the fire. Orlo Williams, *Life and Letters of John Rickman*, 1911, p. 309.

2 Prayers in the House of Commons

1 The first recorded meeting of the Commons in the Abbey was in 1256 in the Chapter House. Charles H. Parry, *Parliaments and Councils of England chronologically arranged from the reign of William I to the Revolution in 1668*, 1839, p. 37.

2 There were forty-nine monks in 1303. E. H. Pearce, *The Monks of Westminster*, 1916, p. 11.

3 Rosser, *op. cit.*, p. 252. See also Harvey, *op. cit.*, p. 45 ff.

4 Philip Laundy, 'Prayers in Parliament' in *Parliamentary Affairs*, (the Journal of the Hansard Society for Parliamentary Government), vol. xi, 1957–58, p. 425 and Norman Wilding and Philip Laundy, *Encyclopedia of Parliament*, 1972, p. 568, says that in the early days of parliamentary history the work of the session was preceded by Mass, usually in the Chapel of St Stephen. Later when the two Houses separated, the custom was kept up, the practice in Tudor times being for the House of Lords to attend service in the Abbey and for the Commons to resort to St Margaret's Church.

5 Arthur Irwin Dasent, *The Speakers of the House of Commons from the Earliest Times to the Present Day with a Topographical Description of Westminster at Various Epochs and a Brief Record of the Principal Constitutional Changes during Seven Centuries*, 1909, pp. 342–376.

6 *De Predicatione ad Parliamentum*, x, 15–24, *Modus Tenendi Parliamentum* in Nicholas Pronay and John Taylor, *Parliamentary Texts of the Later Middle Ages*, 1980, p. 71 (trans. p. 84).

7 'The parliament shall begin at Prime time, because divine service should first be heard'. 'Tracts prior to the Reign of Queen Elizabeth. The manner of holding Parliaments in the Reign of Richard the second. Copied from an ancient manuscript' in ed. Walter Scott, *Somers Tracts*, vol. i, 2nd ed., 1809, p. 7.

8 James Gairdner, *History of Richard III*, 1878, pp. 195–6.

9 There is a bald statement, 'The first prayer that was said in the House of Commons was in anno 1 Hen IV' (i.e. 1461) in Ambrose Kelly text, a compilation by a late seventeenth century Under Clerk employed by the Clerk of the House which he completed in 1685. Behind part of the collection is a text of 1581. (See ed. W. R. McKay, *Observations, Rules and Orders of the House of Commons*, House of Commons Library Documents No. 17, 1989, p. 173).

10 *CJ*, i, 54; *D'Ewes Journal*, p. 47. The Litany was presumably that of the 1552 Prayer Book. That book provides 'the Letanye to be used upon Sundayes, Wednesdayes and Fridayes and at other times', F. E. Brightman, *The English Rite*, vol. i, 1915, p. 175.

11 *CJ*, i, 82.; *D'Ewes Journal*, p. 83 has 'the Prayer which shall begin at eight of the Clock'.

12 Dasent, *op. cit.*, p. 162.

13 *DNB*, vol. xii, p. 221.

14 'Account of a manuscript, by Thomas Norton, Member of Parliament for, and Remembrancer to, the City of London, relating to the ancient duties of the Lord Mayor and Corporation, in a letter from J. PAYNE COLLIER, Esq., Vice-President, to THOMAS LOTT, Esq., F.S.A.', *Archaelogia*, xxxvi, pt. i, pp. 103–104.

15 E.g. *CJ*, i, 118, 150, 266, 353. On 23 Jan. 1580 'for shortness of time the litany was omitted and the prayers only read by the Speaker'. This was due to the late arrival of the Speaker. *ibid*, i, 118.

16 W. R. McKay, *Clerks in the House of Commons 1363–1989: A Biographical List*, House of Lords Record Office Occasional Publications No. 3, 1989, p. 77.

17 *CJ*, i, 150.

18 *D'Ewes Journal*, p. 349.

19 *Ibid*, pp. 566, 567.

20 *Ibid*, p. 661.

21 *CJ*, i, 640.

22 *CJ*, vi, 440.

23 *CJ*, vii, 366.

24 A. Tindal Hart, 'The Abomination of Desolation' in ed. Edward Carpenter, *A House of Kings. The History of Westminster Abbey*, revised ed. 1980, pp. 170–73.

25 'St Olave . . . was one of the parishes in which radical and violent iconoclastic actions took place at the very beginning of the revolutionary era. Although not an important parochial community in the City, some of its civic leaders were at times deeply involved in both religion and politics in Puritan London'. Tai Liu, *Puritan London, A Study of Religion and Society in the City Parishes*, Delaware, Newark, 1986, pp. 43, 127.

26 *CJ*, vii, 595.

27 *Ibid.*, vii, 644.

28 *The Parliamentary Intelligencer*, from 7 May to 14 May 1660, 20, 306.

29 A. G. Matthews, *Calamy Revised, being a revision of Edmund Calamy's Account of the Ministers and others rejected and silenced, 1660–7*, 1934, pp. 67–8. For Calamy see *DNB*, vol. iii, p. 683 ff.

30 *The Diurnall Occurances of Dayly Proceedings of Both Houses, in this Great and Happy Parliament from the third of November 1640 to the third of November 1641 with a continuation of all speeches from June last, to the third of November 1641*, 1641 (*Peel Tracts*, vol. 101) p. 4. Jeremiah 50.5: 'They shall inquire concerning Zion with their faces thitherward, saying, Come ye, and join yourselves to the Lord in an everlasting covenant that shall not be forgotten'. 2 Chronicles 2.3: 'And Solomon sent to Hiram the King of Tyre, saying, As thou didst deal with David my father, and didst send him cedars to build an house to dwell therein, even so deal with me'. For Burgess and Marshall see Anne Laurence, *Parliamentary Army Chaplains 1642–1651*, Royal Historical Society Studies in History 59, pp. 106–7 and 151–2.

31 *Loc. cit.*

32 See pp. 23 *infra*.

33 *Diurnall, op. cit*, p. 333.

34 *CJ*, xiii, 162.

35 *Ibid.*, xxiv, 272.

36 *Ibid.*, xiii, 162.

37 Charles Smyth, *Church and Parish, Studies in Church Problems Illustrated from the Parochial History of St Margaret's, Westminster*. The Bishop Paddock Lectures for 1953–4, 1955, p. 26. The standard of preaching, certainly in the early days, was presumably high. Four times Dr Tillotson (1630–94) was invited of whom a contemporary said, 'He was not only the best preacher of the age, but seemed to have brought preaching to perfection'. *Bishop Burnet's History of His Own Times*, vol. ii, 1734, p. 135. Another preacher was Francis Atterbury (1633–1732) of whom Johnson when questioned about the best English Sermons for style said, 'Yes, Sir, one of the best'. *Boswell's Life of Johnson*, ed. G. B. Hill, revised by L. F. Powell, 1934–50; 1964, vol. iii, p. 247.

38 *Miscellaneous Works of Edward Gibbon, Esq.*, 1814, vol. ii, p. 78.

39 *CJ*, lv, 245; *ibid.*, lvi, 33.

40 Typescript list compiled by John Sainty.

3 The appointment of a Chaplain and his reward

1 Josef Redlich, *The Procedure of the House of Commons. A study of its History and Present Form*, 1908, vol. ii, p. 179.

2 *CJ*, viii, 155.

3   '£120 conferred on Mr. Edward Voyce for his Pains and diligent service in constant praying with this House every morning since the beginning of this Parliament'. *CJ*, viii, 229.

4   W. R. McKay, *Secretaries to the Speaker*, House of Commons Library Document No. 14, 1986, pp. 11–23 and McKay, *Clerks, op. cit.*, pp. 82–3.

5   *Select Committee on the Establishment of the House*, Parliamentary Papers, 1833 (HC648), vol. xii. p. 295 (paras 1827–1834) (cf *HC Deb*, 3rd Series, xxvi, 602). Stalls at the places mentioned provided generous financial benefits to the holders.

6   See pp. 30 *infra*.

7   *CJ*, x, 533.

8   *Fasti Wynd.*, p. 49.

9   *Al. Oxon.* (1), vol. ii, p. 544.

10 Dean of Rochester, *FEA*, vol. ii, p. 579.

11 Dean of Windsor 1709, Bishop of Chichester 1709. *Fasti Wynd.*, p. 49.

12 *DNB*, vol. xx, p. 922.

13 *DNB*, vol. xx, p. 922.

14 Speaker 1770–1780 (Dasent, *op. cit.*, pp. 396–9).

15 Egerton Brydges, *Autobiography*, vol. 1, 1834, pp. 39–40. For Brydges see *MEB*, i, 456.

16 Frere went to Westminster as a Canon in 1838, *Al. Cant.* (2), vol. ii, p. 580.

17 *Select Committee on Establishment of the House of Commons 1833*.

18 *HC Deb*, 3rd Series, xxvi. 603.

19 4th William IV and 1st Victoria.

20 *Al. Cant.* (2), vi, 276. Nor did any of the Chaplains subsequently. See Part 2, pp. 57 ff. *infra*.

21 Reginald Farrar, *The Life of Frederic William Farrar*, 1904, p. 232.

4   The task of the Chaplain in more recent times

1   *CJ*, viii, 155.

2   *CJ*, viii, 388.

3   See art. 'Parson', *ODCC* (ed. 2), p. 1035.

4   *GM*, (1793), lxiii, 418–9. Further evidence for this incident is in *The Shorthand Diary of the Revd Joseph Price*, 1770, p. 31 (Public Library, Canterbury): 'Barford turned out by Norton of St John's in this University. The Speaker absolutely makes the Chaplain, but it has been thought that when appointed the House is so much in possession of him that the Speaker cannot displace him without consulting the House. Restored and King, who married Norton's sister, sent back to the North again'.

5   Philip Marsden, *The Officers of the Commons, 1363–1978*, 1979, pp. 147 and 174.

6   *Ibid.*, p. 176.

7   Arnold Wilson, 'Parliament at Prayers', *The Nineteenth Century*, April 1937, p. 20.

8   Mr. Speaker Weatherill's letter to present incumbent (quoted by permission): 'As you know, I attach importance to the pastoral side of the duties of the Speaker's Chaplain and I have a concern for the welfare of those who live and work here. They number 3,500 all told and a further 4,000 have regular access to the building, so we are quite a large community'.

9   *Liber Niger Quaternus* (a 15th century compilation), *WAM*, Book 1, f. lxxvj. b.

10 *CJ*, i, 140.

11 *CJ*, i, 457, 463.

12 'Westminster Church' is Westminster Abbey. *CSPD*, James 1, 1611–18, p. 231.

13 'For auoyding of all matters and occasion of discencion, it is mete that the bread prepared for the Comunion, be made through all this realme, after the sorte and fashion: that is to say, unleavened and rounde, as it was afore, but without any maner of printe'. Brightman, *op. cit.*, vol. ii, p. 716.

14 R. M. Woolley, *The Bread of the Eucharist*, Alcuin Tracts xi, 1913, pp. 38–43.

15 *CJ*, i, 463.

16 E.g. *D'Ewes Journal*, 5 Nov., 18 Dec., 1641. See also *Mercurius Politicus*, Feb. 23–Mar. 1, 1659; *Mercurius Publicus*, April 19–26, 1660.

17 Charles Smyth, (Rector of St Margaret's 1945–1956) *Church and Parish, op. cit*, p. 21. See also for a discussion on the way in which the Communion was used by the House of Commons not only as a sign of unity, but also as a Sacramental test. *ibid.*, p. 7 ff. Pepys records on 26 May 1661, "This day the Parliament received the Communion of Dr Gunning at St Margaret's, Westminster." *The Diary of Samuel Pepys*, ed. Robert Latham and William Matthews, 1970, vol. ii, p. 107.

18 Mackenzie E. C. Walcott, *History of the Parish Church of Saint Margaret in Westminster from its foundation AD 1064*, 1847, p. 10.

19 *Ibid.*, pp. 107–116.

20 H. E. Westlake, *St Margaret's Westminster. The Church of the House of Commons*, 1914, pp. 106–111.

21 Hilary Wayment, 'The East Window of St Margaret's Westminster', *Antiquaries Journal*, vol. lxi, pt. 2, 1981, pp. 292–301.

22 *House Magazine*, vol. 10, no. 285, 23 November, 1984; *ibid.*, vol. 12, no. 375, 24 November, 1986.

23 William Maitland and others, *The History and Survey of London from its Foundation to the Present Times*, 1756, vol. ii, p. 1339. This is the original source of a quotation often mistakenly attributed to *CJ* in 1735.

24 G. J. Cuming, *History of Anglican Liturgy*, 2nd ed., 1982, p. 151.

25 There is a description of the service in Thomas Archer, *Queen Victoria: her life and Jubilee*, vol. iv, 1888, pp. 219–25.

26 *CJ*, clii, 293.

27 *Ibid*, 322.

28 G. K. A. Bell, *Randall Davidson Archbishop of Canterbury*, 3rd ed., 1952, vol. ii, p. 916. The House had attended a special service of intercession on 4 August 1918 at a very crucial juncture in the Great War at which the King and Queen were also present. Note: 'The House of Commons and St Margaret's Church' at the beginning of *St Margaret's Church Westminster Parochial Church Council Minute Book, 1922–1975*. *WAM* (St Margaret's Papers).

29 Smyth, *Church and Parish, op. cit.*, p. 32.

30 *Al. Cant.* (1), vol. iii, p. 8.

31 *Al. Oxon.* (2), vol. iv, p. 1518.

32 *Ecclesiastical Commissioners Act 1840*.

33 Farrar, *op. cit.*, p. 232. It is said that White conducted a thousand weddings during his 31 years at the Savoy. *MEB*, iii, pp. 1311–2.

34 *Ibid.*, p. 313.

35 G. W. E. Russell, *Basil Wilberforce, A Memoir*, 1917, pp. 97–8.

36 *WWW*, (1929–40), pp. 222–3.

37 G. H. Harris, *Vernon Faithful Storr, A Memoir*, 1943, p. 82.

38 Cheshire: *The Times*, 21 Oct 1958; Campbell: *WWW*, (1961–70), p. 175. See also Roger

Lloyd, *The Church of England, 1900–1965,* 1966, p. 580: 'the cause of the Kingdom was notably served by Canon McLeod Campbell . . . for year after year he wrote a series of outstandingly good reports.'

39 *WWW,* (1971–80), p. 578.

40 *WW,* (1990), p. 543.

41 *Westminster Abbey and Saint Margaret Westminster Act 1972,* Cap xxvi.

42 *Ibid.,* part ii, 6(2).

43 Canon Charles Smyth wrote, on his appointment as Rector of St Margaret's, to Speaker Clifton-Brown that he would not wish to be considered for appointment as Chaplain on health grounds. (Letter: Canon Charles Smyth to Speaker, 24 July 1946. In File 'Speaker's Chaplain', Speaker's Office).

44 p. 22 *supra.*

45 *The Diary of Sir Courtenay Ilbert,* 3 February 1906. *HLRO,* MS.70. I am grateful to Mr W. R. McKay for directing my attention to this entry.

46 Viscount Ullswater, *A Speaker's Commentaries,* 1925, vol. ii, pp. 33–5.

47 Russell, *Wilberforce, op. cit.*

48 *Church of England Assembly (Powers) Act 1919.* (9 and 10 Geo. v cap 76).

49 Leaflet pasted in *Minute Book, op. cit., WAM* (St Margaret's Papers).

50 Letter of Canon W. H. Carnegie and Sir Edward Coates MP, April 1921. *WAM* (St Margaret's Papers).

51 Leaflet 'The St Margaret's Parliamentary Church Council: its Constitution and Purposes', n.d., *WAM* (St Margaret's Papers).

52 *Minute Book, op. cit.*

53 *Westminster Abbey and Saint Margaret Westminster Act 1972, op. cit.*

54 *Ibid.,* (12) a, *passim.*

55 *Ibid.,* Part iv, 19.

56 *Ibid.,* Part iv, 18.

57 170 *HC Deb.* (5th ser.) 170, col. 1928 (10 March 1924).

58 *Ibid.,* cols. 2092–4.

59 Westlake, *St Margaret's, op. cit.*

60 *The Times,* Wednesday 12 March 1924, p. 13.

61 Correspondence in the files of the Gentleman Usher of the Black Rod, House of Lords. See also the statement made by Canon Carnegie to the Parliamentary Church Council on February 26th 1925. *Minute Book, op. cit.*

62 HC Deb. (5th ser.) vol. 189 col. 955 (14 December 1925). See also John Biggs-Davison and George Chowdharay-Best, *Catholic Companion to the Houses of Parliament,* 1990, pp. 12–14.

63 It is said that the first celebration of the Holy Communion in the Chapel after the restoration following the 1834 fire was on 26 June 1911. It was celebrated by Archdeacon Wilberforce on the occasion of the Golden Wedding of Sir David and Lady Erskine. Sir David was Deputy Serjeant-at-Arms (1875–1885) and Serjeant-at-Arms (1885–1915). Ed. Mrs Stewart Erskine, *The Memoirs of Sir David Erskine, KCVO,* 1926, p. 180.

64 *Houses of Parliament Christian Fellowship Minute Book.*

65 *House Magazine,* vol. 14, no. 452, July 17 1989, p. 23.

66 Private circular.

5 Daily Prayers in the House of Commons

1 *CJ*, i, 118.

2 Quoted in Arnold Wright and Philip Smith, *Parliamentary Past and Present*, vol. 11, n.d. (c 1900) and, following them, it is repeated in Laundy, *Prayers, op. cit.*, p. 426. Wright and Smith do not give the source of the text and Mr Laundy, in a private communication (July 1990), was unable to throw any further light on the problem.

3 *D'Ewes Journal*, p. 551.

4 Philip Laundy, *The Office of Speaker*, 1964, p. 185.

5 *CJ*, i, 150.

6 *Ibid.*, i, 266.

7 *Ibid.*, i, 353.

8 *Ibid.*, viii, 176.

9 *Ibid.*, i, 713.

10 For the full text see Appendix I, pp. 81–2 *infra*.

11 *ODCC* (ed. 2) p. 86; Alan Campbell Don, *The Scottish Book of Common Prayer 1929*, 1949, p. 17 ff.

12 See Brightman, *op. cit.*, vol. 1, p. clxvii and Frank Streatfeild, *The State Prayers and other Variations in the Book of Common Prayer*, 1950, pp. 14–15.

13 Streatfeild, *op. cit.*, p. 16.

14 C. Leo Berry, '. . . and all the Royal Family', *History Today*, vol. xvi, April 1966, pp. 176–7; A. W. S. Brown, 'The Prayer Books in the Choir of St George's Chapel', *Annual Report of the Friends of St George's Chapel*, (to 31 December 1957), pp. 20–29.

15 Lord Hemingford, *Backbencher and Chairman*, 1946, pp. 44–5.

16 pp. 39–42 *supra*.

17 J. H. Blunt, *Annotated Book of Common Prayer*, 1844, p. 237.

18 E.g. Dasent, *op. cit.*, p. 159.

19 W. E. Scudamore, *Notitia Eucharistica*, 2nd and revised ed., 1872, p. 716.

20 *The First and Second Prayer Books of Edward VI*, ed. D. E. W. Harrison, 1968, p. 228.

21 Thomas Fuller, *The Church History of Britain*, 1652, Bk. vii, p. 386. There are interesting discussions on the subject of the evidence for Cranmer's involvement in E. C. Ratcliff, 'The Liturgical Work of Archbishop Cranmer', *Journal of Ecclesiastical History*, vol. vii, (1956), pp. 189–203 (which is reprinted in eds. A. H. Couratin and D. H. Tripp, *E. C. Ratcliff Liturgical Studies*, 1976, pp. 184 ff) and in C. W. Dugmore, 'The First Ten Years 1549–59' in *The English Prayer Book 1549–1662*, Alcuin Tract xxxiv, 1963, pp. 6–30.

22 Ed. W. K. Clay, *Liturgies and Occasional forms of Prayer set forth in the reign of Queen Elizabeth*, Parker Society ed., 1847, p. 17.

23 See p. 42 *supra*.

24 See p. 49 *infra*.

25 *Erskine May*, (21st ed.), p. 167.

26 *CJ*, ii, 36. See also the discussions as to whether a member must be present for the whole of Prayers to claim his seat in John Hatsell, *Precedents*, 1818, p. 93.

27 Berry, *op. cit., passim*.

28 For early history of prayers in the House of Lords see E. R. Foster, *The House of Lords 1603–1649*, p. 22.

29 In 1970 he had the choice of Psalms 24, 46, 67, 93 and 111; since 1979 Psalms 1, 15, 24,

34 (vv. 1–8), 46, 66 (vv. 1–14, 18), 67, 93, 95 (vv. 1–7), 100, 111, 112 (vv. 1–6), 119 (vv 34–40), 121, 145 (vv. 1–6). *Companion to Standing Orders of the House of Lords*, Appendix F, 'Prayers for Parliament', pp. 214–5.

30 Letter: Speaker's Secretary (N. E. V. Short) to Speaker's Chaplain (T. S. Nevill), 24 April 1970.

31 See p. 49–50 *infra* for the private nature of Prayers. Also *Erskine May*, (21st ed.), p. 275, f.n. 2.

32 *HC Deb (5th ser.), rol. 478 col. 2929.*

33 *Ibid.*, cols. 2929–2930.

34 *Seventh Centenary of Simon de Montfort's Parliament, 1265–1965. An Account of the Commemorative Ceremonies and an Historical Narrative*, pt. 1, p. 16.

35 Nevill succeeded Stancliffe as Chaplain in 1969 (see part 2).

36 *Account, op. cit.*, p. 13.

37 Full details of the procession are given in Peter Thorne, *Ceremonial and the Mace in the House of Commons*, House of Commons Library Document No. 11, 1980, pp. 1–4.

38 Thus Members, Officers and Staff can call on the Chaplain in complete confidentiality without going through Speaker's Office.

39 Thorne, *op. cit.*, p. 51.

40 The 'Geneva Gown' is the source of disagreement among the authorities. It is argued that a gown is an integral part of clerical dress from before the Reformation. 'Gowns come to us from the Middle Ages; and the Priest's Gown – so far from having anything to do with Geneva – was as bitterly opposed by the Puritans as the cope or surplice'. Percy Dearmer, *Ornaments of the Ministers*, new ed., 1920, pp. 121–123. H. J. Clayton, *Cassock and Gown*, Alcuin Club Tract no. xviii, 1929, p. 12 gives details of 17th century Visitation Articles on the subject. Clayton (*ibid.*, p. 10) maintains that the Puritan dress was a cloak rather than a gown.

41 Dearmer, *Ornaments, op. cit.*, p. 121 (see also plate 39).

42 Many examples of the custom of bowing to the altar continuing into the late 17th century are given in J. Wickham Legg, *English Church Life from the Restoration to the Tractarian Movement considered in some of its neglected or forgotten features*, 1914, pp. 177–180; see also J. O. Coop, Art. 'Bowing' in ed. George Harford, Morley Stevenson and J. W. Tyrer, *Prayer Book Dictionary*, n.d. (1919?).

43 *Erskine May*, (21st ed.), p. 275.

44 *HC Deb* (6th ser.) vol. 158, col. 1.

45 p. 43 *supra*.

PART TWO

Introduction

1   *Hearne*, i, p. 221.

2   Quoted in F. R. Raines, Introduction to Gastrell's *Notitia Cestriensis, Chetham Society Remains*, 1850, p. xliv.

3   *Hearne*, i, p. 231.

4   *DNB*, vol. xii, p. 227.

5   *Hearne*, i, p. 397.

6   *Ibid.*, i. p. 221.

7   *Ibid.*

8   Gordon Rupp, *Religion in England, 1688–1791*, 1986, pp. 499 ff.

9   A. Tindal Hart, *Curate's Lot, the story of the unbeneficed English clergy*, 1970, *passim*.

10 Chadwick, *op. cit.*, vol. i, p. 136 ff.

11 Diana McClatchey, *Oxfordshire Clergy 1777–1869*, 1960, p. 49.

12 *GM*, (1843), cxxiii, p. 103.

13 *Al. Cant.* (1), vol. i, p. 223.

14 *Nov. Rep.*, pp. 114, 449.

15 *GM*, (1859), vii (n.s.), (2), p. 426.

16 Westlake, *op. cit.*, p. 233.

17 *GM*, (1831) ci, (1), p. 186.

18 *DNB*, vol. xiii, p. 1079.

19 *Endymion*, bk. i, ch. 4.

20 R. D. Burnell, *Oxford and Cambridge Boat Race 1829–1953*, 1954, p. 25 (see also p. 163.)

21 *Wordsworth*, p. 56.

22 Christopher Dodd, *Oxford and Cambridge Boat Race*, 1983, pp. 15, 356, 367.

23 *ROW*, ii, p. 943.

24 See art. 'Children's Literature' in ed. Margaret Drabble, *Oxford Companion to English Literature*, 5th ed., 1985, pp. 192–3.

25 *DNB, (1971–1980)*, p. 578.

26 See Farrar, *op. cit.*, *passim*.

27 *DNB*, vol. iii, pp. 291–2.

28 Stratford's father became Bishop of Chester, Manningham (the younger) father became Bishop of Chichester and Moss's Bishop of Bath and Wells.

29 *WWW*, (1929–40), 222.

30 *Hearne*, i, p. 82.

31 *Ibid.*

32 *GM*, (1835), iii (n.s.), p. 554.

Appendix II

1 Jerold J. Savory, *The "Vanity Fair" Gallery – A Collector's Guide to the Caricatures*, South Brunswick USA, 1979, pp. 17–21.

2 *Vanity Fair*, 26 December 1874, Men of the Day no. xclv. See p. xxx, *supra*.

3 Savory, *op. cit.*, p. 24.

4 *Vanity Fair*, 18 October 1879, Men of the Day no. 207. See p. xxx, *supra*.

5 Leslie Ward, *Forty Years of 'Spy'*, new ed. 1917, p. 245.

6 *Vanity Fair*, 10 October 1891, Men of the Day no. 320. See p. xxx, *supra*.

7 *Ibid.*, 6 January 1900, Men of the Day no. mclii. See p. xxx, *supra*.

8 Ward, *op. cit.*, pp. 245–6.

General Index

Illustration references are printed in *italic*

Index of Speaker's Chaplains

Printed in the United Kingdom for HMSO
Dd 0506185   5/91   C7   3382   4235   121707   Job Number 902896